Building Your Farm Legacy:

...tools to empower
better family communication

Elaine Froese, CSP, CAFA
Canada's Farm Whisperer

ISBN-13: 978-1546821243
ISBN-10: 1546821244

TABLE OF CONTENTS

DEDICATION

For Wes, loving husband, compassionate mentor and founder

For Ian and Kendra, servant-hearted successor team

For Erica, loving non-farm heir

For Penny Grace, our granddaughter, the future generation

For all legacy builders

ACKNOWLEDGEMENT AND THANKS

To Carolyn Crummey and her Virtasktic team for crafting seven years of writing into this book. Carolyn's skills empower me to have sacred space and time with farm families to deepen my impact.

To Susan Armstrong at Grainews and Tom Button and Maggie Van Camp at Country Guide for their decades of support, editing and encouragement.

To the transparent farm families who share their struggles and healing stories with me as we all work together to find clarity of expectations, certainty of timelines and a commitment to act to build a healthy culture in agriculture and an amazing legacy for our families.

Preface

Throughout the past 32 years, I have been a guest in thousands of farm homes across the prairies. It has also been a special honor to be present in print form in the farm paper columns of *"Grainews,"* giving seeds of encouragement to my tribe. Now I offer you this book: a collection of the last six years of my journey.

I am a farm family coach, owner of a farm business, spouse to the farm manager, mother to the successor, and a mother-in-law. Like you, I have multiple roles in my southwestern Manitoba seed farm and a need for harmony and connection to my team.

I hope these stories and insights give you a sense of hope and thankfulness for this great culture of agriculture. I also hope that you will glean wisdom, process new ideas, and courageously act on what you know needs to happen next.

My vision is to empower family, increase profit and secure legacy.

We reap what we sow; let's all work at leaving a loving legacy to our farm families!

Enjoy, and let me know what you think at www.elainefroese.com/contact.

Introduction:
12 Phrases That Will Help You
Take Charge of Your Farm

One snowy day at a beautiful ranch home in southern Alberta around the expansive kitchen table, the farm team said, "Elaine you should make a list of your top phrases that you use in coaching." "Okay," I said, knowing that many of the best projects are started by attentive practical ranchers and farmers who call it as they see it.

12 Important Phrases for Farmers

It is your farm. Your family. Your choice.

This is my essential message as a coach. I want farm folks to build new scenarios for the new chapters in their lives that suit their values and goals. Many folks who feel "stuck" have not stopped to talk with themselves about what they really want in their life, their family and their farm business. Are you sensing a new chapter coming up in your life? What choices do you have to make some new experiences happen?

You get the behavior you accept.

So why are you putting up with bad behavior? Folks, you do not have to allow abuse, profanity, or nasty behavior on your farm. Stand up for what you believe is right. Find support beyond your farm gate.

That was then, and this is now.

(Attributed to my mother-in-law, Margaret Froese). Meaning that things change and you might need to make a new decision for the present and the future. Some founders make promises to successors that have to be broken when the financial reality dictates that the founders need more money for their re-invention years. Plans can change, but the basic trust doesn't need to be harmed if the parties can all be honest, transparent, and agree to talk about their disappointment.

A farm is not a piece of pie.

This means the critical mass of assets needs to stay with the farm owner or shareholders. Create another wealth bubble for your non-business heirs or have great agreements that allow access to the land for the farm operation. Parents are not responsible for ensuring that all of their adult children are economically equal. Many adult children have wealth creation goals that don't demand large gifts from hard-working founders. Perhaps if you sat down with your children, you'd discover that their primary desire is for you to have some rewards now and to be able to enjoy the fruit of your labor.

Change is inevitable; growth is optional.

Change is going to happen, but are you ready to embrace it and work through the necessary steps to achieve your goals in a timely fashion and meet the needs of your team? The Hudson Institute gave me a great map called the "cycle of renewal" that helps families navigate change and make mini-transitions to become aligned again with their vision and goals. Life is not a straight line, and we are more resilient to the bumps in the road when we take a "learner" approach.

You are good enough.

This is a take on Brene Brown's work where she says, "You are enough."

Many young farmers feel that no matter how hard they work it is never "good enough." All of our farms could use more intentional affirmation. Lately, I have been asked to speak about "encouraging the heart of your farm." We all need more affirmation and appreciation on our farm teams.

Divorce on farms does not have to happen.

This saying provoked a profane outburst at one of my seminars, but I meant it. Love and respect for all players and spouses on your farm will go a long way to avoiding the divorce courts. Sometimes I think people don't ask for professional help soon enough, and then the pain and wounds are far too deep to be healed.

When is it her turn to get what she needs?

This is the uncomfortable question posed to the aging founder who has been married for over 45 years and still cannot see what his wife is longing for in a new chapter of life beyond the farm. She wants to move away from the main yard (Grand Central Station) and spend more time with her hobbies and friends in town. She is tired. She knows her husband still wants a role on the farm, but now it needs to be different as the next generation becomes the main manager.

A conversation is not a contract.

My friend Jolene Brown likely coined this term first, and she is right. Many promises as conversations will not hold up when challenged. Families in business are wise to write things down in agreements that keep a record of what was decided and promised.

Love does not read minds.

I think I was told this as a young bride by our minister, and I used this phrase recently in a coaching call. It was powerful when I saw the young farmer's binder page with the quote in BOLD block letters. He is planning to make it into a wooden plaque for his kitchen.

You have options; you can leave.

A young frustrated farm woman asked me in a seminar Q&A what to do with a father-in-law who was not treating her with respect. I quickly said, "Just leave." She did not leave, but the notion that she did have the option to choose a different path gave her the freedom to make her current situation different. She now blogs about agriculture, and we had the pleasure of reuniting a few months ago. I had no idea of the power of the phrase until she told me her story. You can find out more about "necessary endings" in our book *Farming's In-law Factor.* Chapter ten talks about what to do when things don't work out.

Conflict resolution is a business risk management strategy. Discuss the Undiscussabull™.

I believe that conflict avoidance is one of the huge boulders holding agriculture back. Many founders have a fear of conflict, so they procrastinate and do not have courageous conversations. I've coined the term "undiscussabull" as the bull in the middle of the room that everyone knows is there, but they continue to avoid talking about it. Attack an issue without attacking the person, and get resolution. Don't waste emotional energy on "drama." Learn to focus on solving problems with effective, focused management.

About This Book

The chapters of this eBook explore many of these important phrases, with personal stories, actionable advice, and tips that will help you improve life on the farm. From relationships, habits, and communication to operations, planning, and succession, my ultimate goal is for you to develop new strategies that strengthen your farm and family, and help you enjoy a rewarding career as a farmer.

If you are like me, you might want to pick up a pen and scribble notes at the back or in the margins. Marking up books is a learning process for me, where I write important lessons down in the margins and take note of my favorite page numbers at the back so I can find them again for easy reference.

RELATIONSHIPS

Chapter 1:

9 Tips on How to Love a Farmer

"Elaine is a marriage counselor, even though she says she is a coach!" says the uncomfortable farmer after a coaching call. I tell my clients that "counseling is about recovery, but coaching is about discovery." I want farm couples to discover what will work for them to be happier in their relationship as a couple, and as farm partners. Sometimes I ask hard questions that irk people, but they know they need to deal with making their marriage foundation stronger.

In John Gottman's book, *The 7 Principles for Making a Marriage Work* he talks about developing a friendship in your marriage and learning to make repairs. With this in mind, here are some of my top tips on how to love a farmer.

9 Tips on How to Love a Farmer

1. Respect Him. Respect Her.

Author Emmerson Eggerichs (Love and Respect) has suggested that in a relationship, men are looking for respect and women need love. I suspect that your spouse needs to hear words of affirmation from you that you are "proud of them and appreciate their character and decision-making ability." Filling up the emotional bank account for each person in your family just takes courage to speak truth and love into the other person's life. Be intentional about doing it, not just on special occasions. Do you currently show respect to your farmer?

2. Cook

"A Hot Meal" is on the top of my farmer's caring list. We took the time to explore the 12 ways we each like to be cared for, wrote it down, and laughed. Wes feels deeply loved when he walks into the house and can smell something good stewing. Only 21 percent of Canadians still cook from scratch, so affirm your cooking skills and show them off to your family. When was the last time you cooked your hubby's favorite supper? He cares. You can also love your farmer by cooking healthy foods and not stuffing him full of sugary sweets. Love your physical hearts with smart cooking. I also realize that many women farmers are happy to have spouses who cook for them, too!

3. Time

Smalley and Trent use the concept of "word pictures" to convey strong meaning in marriage. When Wes reports that he feels he is getting "leftovers" he is telling me I am spending more energy on my clients, readers, and audience than on him. I do not like to hear about this kind of leftovers, so I need to check in and ask how he is doing regarding the time we are spending together, enjoying each other and being connected. Quality time is one of the five love languages that Gary Chapman writes about. Are you spending more time with grandchildren and neglecting the time needs of your spouse? Could you block off, at least, one hour a week as "marriage time" to work on the state of your union? Walk. Date. Talk.

4. Service

Someone suggested that "clutter is energy constipation." Our lives can be cluttered with busy activities and taking care of too much stuff. If you are ready to simplify things, how about attacking a project together as a couple. I know a wife who was thrilled to see the ugly old barn burn down (on purpose) as it was part of the view from her home she hated. When I mentioned that the patio furniture needed to be parked away for the winter, I felt deeply loved when that same day the guys hauled it away to the shed on the flatbed. Small acts of kindness really mean a lot to a weary heart. How tidy and clean is your home sanctuary? Clean up together.

Mending is also a sign of love. Patches anyone?

5. Candy Under the Pillow

Do you still know your farmer's favorite treat? Is it licorice, almonds, or chocolate? Keep some on hand to pop into the lunch kits to the field. A small treat communicates "I am thinking of you, and I care about you." (Nuts do not have sugar, just fat, oh well!).

6. Discuss Debt Together

Please talk before spending large sums of money and what impact that will have on the family. Women are tired of off-farm jobs subsidizing the farm cash flow only to discover that their opinion was not brought to the loan negotiating table. Disaster looms when debt is hidden and not openly discussed to explain the "why we are doing this" factors. A young hurting farmer confides that he separated due to a large dairy debt that was not ratified by his wife. She was deeply hurt that she had been kept in the dark. Women, are you using too much "retail therapy" to compensate for marriage deficits? Men, do you have expensive leisure habits that are hurting cash flow?

7. Make Repairs Quickly

Nip conflicts in the bud and don't let stress simmer. Have a 10'clock rule that you will commit to resolving disputes before bedtime so that you can enjoy intimacy and not let the sun set on your anger. Some days you may not be able to fix things in a day, and may then work to agree to "park the issue" until the next business meeting or coffee time.

8. Redemptive Separation

Addictions like alcohol may require time apart for therapy and rehabilitation. The intent of redemptive separation is to practice tough love to get the person you love to change behavior and come back to the marriage in a healthy way. If your marriage is carrying issues that need counseling therapy, a doctor's diagnosis or spiritual care, get help now. I love my farmer so much I check to see if he is keeping up with his medical care. When is the last time you saw your doctor? Do you even have a doctor? Drugs and alcohol are not good stress relievers, they cause more harm and hurt to farm families than many people know.

9. Kiss Often

I do not need to say more.

Have fun loving your farmer and put the "zest" back into your marriage this year. Resiliency for farming starts with a strong marriage foundation. After all, we all want to love and be loved.

Women Are Farmers Too

I've made the above article more inclusive to both spouses since the original version. I recognize that women are farmers, too. The main message is to love and respect your spouse, serving one another to address each other's needs. When the union is strained, pay attention, and work together to get the relationship back on a healthy track.

Notes:

Chapter 2:

Dealing with Sibling Rivalry on the Farm

The longest relationships we have in our lives are typically those with our siblings, which can last 80 years or longer. I heard a radio announcer mention this one day, and then he suggested Dr. Jeanne Safer's book *Cain's Legacy: Liberating Siblings from a Lifetime of Rage, Shame, Secrecy, and Regret.* Wondering what tools Safer has for farm sibling's strife, I bought the book to advise you on how to create better relationships with your siblings.

Parents' Role in Sibling Relationships

"When people have what they need emotionally, they do not envy what others have...even brothers who have cheated them out of what by rights was theirs (Jacob and Esau story)," Safer writes. I wonder if she has ever interviewed the farm sisters who are taking each other to court over dad's will?

Farm families are in deep angst over sibling strife, and you may be shocked at this next observation.

"Parents are responsible for parenting the sibling rivalry that leads to strife and siblings who have a legacy of grief with each other. Parents should not ignore violence or fighting between siblings, and they should defang it. Navigate the wrath!" says Safer.

In my own words, I would say "discuss the undiscussabulls." Deal with the issues when they are small and have the courageous conversation to deal with hostilities before they become entrenched in the family history. If one child is saying, "I am afraid that when our parents die that you'll take everything and not leave anything for me!" then talk about your estates, succession plans, and possession wishes.

Be Conscious

"The most effective strategy is the most elusive: self-knowledge and empathy for all combatants," says Safer. What is it that you really want? Can you evoke some empathy to try and understand what your siblings are going through?

"The best-equipped siblings in strife are those who were well loved themselves (or understand why they weren't) and have satisfying lives." Addressing unfinished business with one's own siblings is the best way to foster mutuality in the next generation.

What Type of Sibling Relationships Are You Modeling?

Do you have an awareness of the conflict and the will to change the future relationships in your family? Many folks I coach are reenacting the past. Safer challenges us to repudiate Cain's legacy (Cain killed his brother Abel in the Bible account). She says that "consciousness and a new perspective on the past will open up for us."

When I work with farm families, I usually ask them to tell me the stories about how the dad and mom got the farm from their parents. I am looking for clues and patterns or perspectives on fairness and keeping the farm intact. Usually, there is a rough relationship between farming brothers, the uncle, and things that the current founders want to avoid with their legacy.

Tips on Coping with Siblings

I am curious if you are courageous enough to be more aware of the internal struggle that your siblings cause in you? Anxiety about knowing and revealing unacceptable feelings (like hate) keeps you stuck and inhibits what you say to your siblings. Likely they already know the truth about how you feel about what is happening.

Could you approach a sibling with: "Let's work on our relationship so that we want to be together?"

Insights to Help You Cope

- **Move on.** This is a coaching term that helps people see that things may never change, so they need to let go and move on. This happens when you create a place of your own while maintaining a very minimal role in your farm family home. Essentially you stay connected in a very small way and build a satisfying life beyond the farm.

- **Reconciliation.** Irreconcilable differences that are beyond repair may teach you to look in the mirror and spare the next generation from the same mistakes. The desire for reconciliation needs to come from both siblings in order to be effective.

- **Branch out.** Adopt a new "family" or find a surrogate family as Safer calls it. We have found our church family to be a part of our extended family, people who chose to love and care for us, even when they are not true relatives. Safer feels that "brotherhood or sisterhood should be earned."

- **Grieve your losses.** What struck me about Safer's insights is that "siblings are indelible, they are written in your heart and your history. Severing your external relationships doesn't mean that you can divest yourself of the internal relationship." So the folks that I meet that have severed physical ties with siblings are still deeply affected by their heart string struggles of wondering what went wrong.

- **Make a choice.** "Whatever decision you make about the type of relationship you will have with a problem sibling, make it a conscious choice; you will have fewer regrets later on. Avoiding the painful truth, blaming external circumstances, letting the relationship trail off, or believing it no longer matters prevents recognition, resolution, and mourning. Acknowledging reality liberates emotional energy, and this will help you discover men and women who can become your authentic psychological

brothers and sisters even if they are not your biological ones."
(Safer, page 211.)

Ten Tips for Moving from Strife

You can recover from the strife you feel from sibling relationships. Here is my advice.

1. Strive to see the world from the other person's perspective.

2. Empathize and appreciate what the other sibling has tried to do. Build on the positive.

3. Explain the "why" or the intent behind estate decisions.

4. Don't let the parents sow the seeds of favoritism.

5. Take initiative to have frequent conversations so that you are not kept apart by silence.

6. Some people love money more than a relationship. Let them go. Money does not buy love. Identify the roles your parents played or contributed to the conflict so you can alter the outcome.

7. Embrace honest conversations. Be real. Hurt siblings need to be validated by being seen and heard before forgiveness comes. Rebuilding trust takes time and self-awareness.

8. Accept "good enough." "Sometimes you have to adjust your notion of the perfect reconciliation to the good-enough one that accepts the other person as she is," says Safer.

9. Seek common ground or common interests, rather than staying stuck in your positions. What is it that you both really want?

10. Take risks to have courageous encounters that build trust. "Your willingness to hear, without becoming defensive, how the other person sees the situation establishes trust, which is the most potent tool for reconciliation," says Safer.

Be receptive to emotional engagement when searching for insights into your sibling strife history. As Dr. Jeanne Safer explains, "The only person whose involvement you can control is yourself." I would add that you might also want to pray for wisdom and divine intervention in the process.

Notes:

_____

_____

_____

_____

_____

_____

_____

_____

_____

_____

Chapter 3:

Father and Son: Advice for Farm Transition Relationships

Another teary-eyed father sits in my coaching session rubbing his face, trying to hide his disappointment. He really wants to get things sorted out with his son, but his emotions are keeping him stuck. When I suggest that all he really wants is to be respected and appreciated for all he and his wife have done, he nods in agreement.

Father's Day on farms is a mixed bag of celebration, avoidance and "let's get back to work!" This year we will all be pressing hard to get the crop in, and hope that nature has a way of compensating delayed seeding. Delays in farm family conversations that embrace the need for affirmation and realistic expectations are not so forgiving.

According to the "Best of the Family Business Advisor" journal from Family Enterprise Publishers, part of succession and personal maturity is "letting go" of the expectations one has towards one's parents. When successors take hold of these four beliefs, they can let go of problematic expectations.

4 Pieces of Advice for Adult Farm Successors

1. Appreciate that your parents are not perfect, and they have made some mistakes in judgment. "Cut them some slack" and model forgiveness.

2. Accept parents for who they are…with respect and love. I am amazed at what I learn about dads in tears when they tell me about difficult sibling partnerships, and addicted fathers, and so on. Everyone's life experience has a back story that gives clues to their fears, dreams, and disappointments.

3. Understand that life is not fair. Cancer, strokes, divorce, heart attacks and accidents that changed your farm's direction are part of the journey of life. Instead of bitterness, how do you choose to make better decisions, and count your blessings?

4. Assume personal responsibility for your own life, security, and identity. It is not the role of parents to make all of their children economically equal. What actions are you taking to be emotionally and financially mature? You can change you. You get the behavior from others that you accept. What do you need and want to do differently?

The Family Business Advisor found that parents' ability to let go of power correlates with the next generation's ability to let go of emotional expectations of their parents. When farm parents see their adult children take personal responsibility for who they are and their own success, the parents can't wait to support the next generation.

"The parents seem to draw on my strength. It helps them," says one successor.

Perfect Gifts for Your Father the Farmer

As you contemplate the perfect gift on Father's Day, it's important to realize that the best gifts are actually intangible.

*   **Grow up.** Show up to the conversation as an adult, not an "entitled child." Work on being more self-reliant, competent, and eager to assume farm business leadership.

*   **Be respectful.** Treat others the way you would like to be treated and stop yelling at each other.

*   **Make repair of the relationship with reconciliation.** Forgive the past mistakes, and clean the slate to make better plans together.

*   **Show verbal appreciation.** Speak words of affirmation to each other.

- **Take time for fun together.** Parents are not usually best friends with their kids, but it does help the emotional bank account of the family to have fun together. What is fun for you?

- **Find the fishing rods, the canoe, the horse tack, or the bikes to create new memories together.** Life will pass by very quickly, and you will never regret the intentional time you take to rally reasonable expectations for being a family, who happen to farm together.

- **Unreasonable expectations are the shortcut to discontent.** Let go of expecting perfection. Embrace the courageous conversations. Enjoy a clearer understanding of what dad and you both need to succeed.

Being a Dad in 2017 is a basket full of roles. You'll find more happiness on the farm when father and successor learn to honor each other.

Notes:

_____

_____

_____

_____

_____

_____

_____

_____

Chapter 4:

Understanding and Encouraging Your Son-In-Law

One of the overlooked team players on the family farm is the son-in-law who is married to the successor, the daughter of the founders. Let's consider some of the dynamics that you need to be aware of to help understand what is going on for the son-in-law (SIL).

Why the SIL Behaves the Way He Does

SILs are often caught between a rock and a hard place. Many are working hard to stay employed on the farm and stay happily married. They are doing their level best to please everyone around them and may deal with this in unhealthy ways, such as drinking or working too much.

When an SIL is directly involved in the farm, he is naturally computing how much he can move things to his favor without risking the chance to be the long-term business partner. He wants to protect his interests and yet be fair to the older generation. He also knows that if he wants his children to be the future heirs of the business, he has to have a viable farm and a legacy of good communication.

The SIL may not have the emotional support system he needs beyond his spouse. His wife is his lover, friend, and business partner, and sometimes mediator. Smart SILs preserve healthy friendships or mentors outside of the farm business, so they have a circle of support beyond the immediate family.

Sometimes SILs do not have the emotional capacity to deal with the frustrations and stress of fitting into a new family business. It can be difficult for them to find resources or a listening ear. It's important that they manage their stress well, or the marriage and their mental health—and ultimately the farm—are at risk of failure.

How Is the SIL Perceived?

The SIL may be embraced as a great asset to the farm and the family, or he may be judged as incompetent (compared to the son of the founder) or deemed not worthy of the daughter that he married.

Each family gets to choose whether they will bless or curse the in-laws.

Divorces on farms do not have to happen; they are the result of choices. The founders' perception and treatment, for example, play a huge part in what is experienced by the SIL. Folks who have their minds already made up about other family members have what I would call "filters of perception" that cloud what they see or limit what they see in the other person. If the SIL is perceived as capable and included in the family without judgment, things are more likely to go well. SILs who are harped on by nasty mother-in-law's (MILs) and father-in-law's (FILs) are at risk of experiencing extreme stress in their marriage.

We all need to be conscious of the biases we are bringing to the table and how we are treating other people. In her book *Change Your Questions, Change Your Life: 10 Powerful Tools for Life and Work*, author Marilee Adams encourages us to have a learner mindset, rather than a judger mindset. She suggests using helpful questions, such as: "What assumptions am I making?" and "What am I responsible for?"

In the web of family relationships, the SIL may find himself caught up in the triangle of indirect communication between the FIL, the MIL, and his wife. He can also find himself compared to the son or in competition with the son. In some instance, it can help to directly address statements or behavior that indicate comparisons with the son are happening. For example, an SIL could say to his FIL, "When you compare me to your son, I feel unappreciated (disrespected, frustrated, etc.) If you have a concern about something I'm doing, I'd gladly discuss it. However, I need the comparisons to stop now."

Some SILs choose not to compete with other family members. Regarding competition, it's hard to run a race against someone who has defaulted the race. You can choose to stop competing. You don't have to keep up with your brother-in-law, other family members, or the Joneses. The SIL can choose to say, "That's fine if that's what you're doing, but I'm going to do my own thing."

Tools for SIL's

- **Self-care:** Making sure that you are taking care of basic physical, emotional, mental health, and social needs. If you are not sleeping well due to stress, have a sleep clinic check you out or seek other treatments.

- **Friendship beyond the farm:** Be sure to set good boundaries for time away. Go hunting, fishing, skiing, etc. with your buddies from high school or college.

- **Honoring the timelines agreed to:** Nail down deadlines at your regular business meetings and have a process for accountability. You might want to engage your accountant or farm coach for accountability.

- **Courageous Conversations:** Make sure conflict is being dealt with openly.

Consider an exit strategy if this doesn't work. What are your options? Update your resume and polish up your marketable skills.

Founders: How to Encourage Your SIL

There are certain questions that founders can ask themselves to evaluate how they are treating the SIL and to forge a better relationship.

- Are we being clear with our expectations?

- Are we economically fair?

- Are we showing appreciation?

- Are we being respectful?

- Can we ask the SIL how things are going for him?

- Are we giving the SIL power to act on things that are important to him?

Having more harmony on family farms means paying attention to better communication and conflict resolution. Release relationship stress by being proactive about how you respect your in-laws and listen for what the other person is needing. Show appreciation to your father and father-in-law. Embrace your son and son-in-law with respect. You'll be amazed what respect and appreciation can do to encourage the heart of your business.

Notes:

_____

_____

_____

_____

_____

_____

_____

_____

_____

Chapter 5:

Tools for In-Law Relationships

In our book *Farming's In-Law Factor*, Dr. Megan McKenzie and I worked on a number of tools to help various in-law relationships on your farm.

On the following pages in this chapter, you'll find question and answer lists that can help you identify the strengths and weaknesses in your current relationship with your in-laws. Use each tool to your advantage by answering the questions honestly. The tools include:

- Founding Generation: Assessment of Daughter-in-Law (DIL) and Son-in-Law (SIL) Relationships

- Next Generation: Assessment of Mother-In-Law (MIL) and Father-In-Law (FIL) Relationships

- Farm Relationship Satisfaction: Self-Assessment Tool

Founding Generation: Assessment of Daughter-in-Law (DIL) and Son-in-Law (SIL) Relationships

1. What new insights or outlooks has our DIL/SIL brought to our family and brought to our farm?

2. What do I most appreciate about our DIL/SIL?

3. What conscious things do we do to embrace our DIL/SIL to make her/him feel loved and accepted?

4. What strengths does she/he offer to our farm team?

5. What has she/he taught me?

6. How has our DIL/SIL shone the light on some of our unwritten family rules or norms?

7. How has our DIL made our son's life better? How has our SIL made our daughter's life better?

8. What do we need to forgive or let go of to make our relationship with our DIL/SIL stronger?

9. What fears has our DIL/SIL helped us to overcome?

10. Three ways that we can show more care for our DIL/SIL are:

11. If I held nothing back, I would tell my DIL/SIL:

12. What sacrifices have we made for the next generation?

Next Generation: Assessment of Mother-In-Law (MIL) and Father-In-Law (FIL) Relationships

1. What do I most appreciate about my MIL? What do I most appreciate about my FIL?

2. What conscious things do we do to embrace our MIL and FIL to make them feel loved and accepted?

3. Three ways that we can show more care for our MIL are to:

4. Three ways that we can show more care for our FIL are to:

5. What has my MIL taught me? What has my FIL taught me?

6. What sacrifices have my in-laws made for me and my spouse?

7. How has your MIL and FIL been a role model for you?

Building Relationships on Family Farms

As we were researching in-law relationships for *Farming's In-Law Factor*, we found that there is very little written about in-law relationship building on family farms. Therefore, we wanted to develop practical tools to help families learn about their values and differences, in order to be more accepting and gracious with each other's strengths and intentions.

Try this chart out and let us know what you think. It is adapted from work in Australia by Mick Faulkner's Agrilink Agricultural Consultants, who I have had the pleasure of working with in the past.

How happy are you with your farm in-laws? And they with you? This is a tool for self-reflection and awareness, and it can also be shared with the farm team.

Farm Relationship Satisfaction: Self-Assessment Tool

Points of Concern	Very Pleased	Pleased	Mostly Satisfied	Mixed	Mostly Dissatisfied	Unhappy	Very Unhappy
I feel accepted by my in-law's.							
I'm able to try new things on the farm.							
There are clear expectations of me.							
We work well to make decisions as a family and I feel my voice is heard.							
The level of criticism in the business is OK.							
I feel that what I do on the farm is valued.							
I feel my investment of labor is turning into equity and/or fair compensation.							
Another important issue for me is:							

Farm Relationship Satisfaction: Analyzing Your Results

If you selected dissatisfied or unhappy for any of these relationship areas, your farm is functioning below its potential.

1. If one or more in-laws feels they are not accepted by their in-laws, this could show a lack of respect or closure of the gate to kinship and being fully included as part of the family.

2. If someone is not able to try new things on the farm, this could be resistance to change, and/or a power imbalance between family members and farm managers.

3. If expectations are unclear, this may be a sign of role confusion, unrealistic expectations and poor communication flooded with assumption.

4. Good decision making allows for all voices to be heard. A lack of this may show a power struggle or poor communication habits. It could be that the "women are to be kept out of business" in some families. Not having a voice can also be a sign of pure disrespect.

5. If a farm family is critical and judgmental, it nurtures destructive behavior and negative workplace culture.

6. Lack of appreciation is a huge stumbling block to business success. This is particularly so for the Generation Y group (born after 1980) who expect more feedback than previous generations do.

7. Financial reward is important for survival and recognition. The goal for most adult children successors or business partners to become owners, and be fairly compensated for their sweat equity and labor.

I am now a mother-in-law (MIL) with a wonderful DIL who is studying hard to become a nurse. You CAN have positive, healthy relationships with your in-laws! Let us all work together towards more harmonious relationships to strengthen our farm teams.

Notes:

_____

_____

_____

_____

_____

_____

_____

_____

_____

_____

Chapter 6:

14 Ways to Help Prevent Divorce on Farms

Each year is a new year of possibilities. Though there may be struggles, there are also opportunities to create a stronger marriage this year and every year.

My parents married December 27, 1955. My brothers each chose to marry that same week in 1984, and 1990. I, being the rebel, got married on Independence Day, July 4, 1981. Wes and I have outlasted Chuck and Di who married the same year, same month.

Divorce is one of the biggest threats to farm family legacy. We need to start talking more about how to prevent the breakups and create more make-ups.

14 Ways to Help Prevent Divorce in Farm Families

As I write this, I am thinking of neighbors, friends, clients of all ages and stages who have struggled to stay married. My prevention list:

1. Ask for What You Need – Love Does Not Read Minds

When I want a hug, I ask. When I need quiet time alone, I negotiate the volume of the TV. My coaching career demands travel and time away; that is okay.

2. Listen to the Needs of the Other and Act

Marriage is not 50/50; it is 100/100. You are committed to serving your mate with a servant attitude, and they serve you. How can you be a better listener? How can you act on what is requested for change? When I talk too much, Wes will squeeze my knee under the table as a loving signal to give others air time. Can you start paraphrasing what your spouse said to make sure you received the message correctly?

3. Be Kind and Respectful

Honey is more appealing than vinegar. Every morning we get to choose if we are kind or nasty in our approach. Grouches need to get checked out by doctors for depression. Most in-laws would never even think of leaving the farm family IF they felt they were respected. What does respect look like to you? Look each other in the eye and ask "How can I show you more respect? What would you like me to do differently?"

4. Walk in Their Boots – Take Another Person's Perspective

Young farmers are craving work/life balance; a chance to read bedtime stories to their kids. Do you remember what it was like to be 35 with young kids? Young moms who work off-farm are exhausted. How can you share the load?

5. Adapt and Yield with "Yes, Dear"

Wes hates putting up Christmas lights, but he still helps me do it. I know he appreciates hot home-cooked meals, so I am happy to vary the menu. There are many ways to accomplish the same goals, which is why I am thankful for frozen stir-fry meals when I am away. Check in with your mate to see if there are other ways to adapt to what they desire.

6. Be Physically Strong and Connected

Yes, we are talking about sex here, and being in shape physically to enjoy the age stage you are at. Many folks are open with me about their sexual frustration; I guess it comes with being a good listener. We all need to love and be loved. Meaningful touch with hugs, kisses, shoulder squeezes is also part of the mix. Don't talk about farming in the bedroom after dark. Play with each other instead.

7. Make Quick Repair

Conflict is normal. Abrasive fighting is bad. John Gottman's book *Seven Principles for Making Marriage Work* is a great read. He emphasizes the need to keep conflicts short and small, then fix them quickly. I say, "extend the olive branch, and reach out to be part of the reconciliation."

8. Be Thankful and Count Your Blessings

Our farming friend has a disabled wife in a wheelchair. They are amazing how they show love to each other. They also remind us that we need to stay committed to each other in sickness and health. Wes has already proven this to me when I spent most of 1984 in the psych ward with a severe post-partum depression. Work on your mental health, and choose a good attitude every day.

9. Reach Out to Quit Your Addictions

We all need support to quit the bad stuff whether you are addicted to work, alcohol, drugs, shopping, or something else. Find counseling, rehab, or a support group to get you to a better place. Anger that is not managed will destroy you and your marriage. Get help.

10. Finish Well Together

Have a lifestyle plan that goes beyond the farm as you age together. Play together. Enjoy grandchildren: please do not ignore these precious little ones. When you die, don't you want to be rich in your relationships? You cannot take your farm shares with you to the grave!

11. Stop Texting, Start Talking Face to Face

Social media is fueling unfaithfulness in marriage. No secret emotional affairs for you. Be open with your mate.

12. Celebrate the Milestones

Give your partner a special card, supper or night out. Bake a cake or pie to share with friends. Strong families celebrate anniversaries, birthdays, weddings, and engagements. Cherish the markers of marriage.

13. Save Sex for Marriage

Don't live together or "shack up" before you have signed your marriage covenant, i.e. wed each other. The stats for the "almost married" common-law unions are pretty sobering. Those folks who live together before marrying are more likely to split. Understand the crudeness of the saying "Why buy the cow when you can get the milk for free?" Your partner may also be happy to look outside your bed for new partners if they did that so easily with you.

14. Fill Each Other's Emotional Bank Account or "Love Tank"

Make deposits every day into the well-being of your spouse. Find out if they like to be loved with words, meaningful touch, gifts, quality time together or acts of service. When was the last time you detailed the pick-up truck? If your guy loves to be loved with action, that will be amazing to him.

I have to stop, but I hope you get the picture. Divorce wreaks havoc in all of our agricultural families. I hurt when I see marriages fail. Let's all work towards encouraging strong unions so that divorce is not a threat to our farm's legacy.

Notes:

_____

_____

_____

_____

COMMUNICATION

Chapter 7:

Farm Team Skills: Forgiveness and Reconciliation

"Man, I can't believe that guy, every time I make a mistake, he just can't accept my apology, and he keeps really good track...for years!"

Does Your Farm Team Have the Ability to Apologize and Forgive?

I was saddened to hear a young farmer confide with me that in all his years, he has never once heard an apology from the farm manager, his father.

Many farm families are saddled with an invisible load on their backs. Every day they carry the baggage of hurt, caused by a habitual pattern of family members who just can't seem to let go of past offenses.

It is time for farm families to learn how to make "quick repair" as John Gottman calls it, and we are not talking about duct tape here! Forgiveness is one of the critical issues that farm families need to take a hard look at. Why do they avoid it?

Accepting the fact that you are hurt is one thing, but the tough part about forgiveness is that it is the offended (you) who has to seek the forgiveness of the offender (another family member). "Forgiveness is difficult because the person who is hurt does the forgiving and *not* the person being forgiven," according to Time Lahaye and Bob Philips, authors of *Anger Is a Choice*.

I was angry with my friend;
I told my wrath; my wrath did end.
I was angry with my foe,
I told it not; my wrath did grow.

-William Blake, A Poison Tree.

We don't forgive and forget. We remember, but we have a choice of what we do with the memories. LaHaye says, "I can let my memories lie and move on in my life, or I can let my memories overpower me. Forgiveness is letting go. It is the relaxation of your death grip on the pain you feel."

Pain and the baggage of hurt from un-forgiveness may be keeping your farm team stuck. You might want to consider the art of surrender. Archibald Hart says, "Forgiveness is surrendering my right to hurt you back if you hurt me."

You choose to forgive; it is an act of the will.

If your farm succession plan is not going well, it might be due to a lack of forgiveness. Tom Hubler of Hubler Family Business Consultants feels that lack of forgiveness is the second biggest obstacle to succession planning. Number one may be stubbornness and pride!

The Reasons for Lack of Reconciliation Are Many

To be able to forgive, we have to look issue of hurt directly. There are many reasons why people choose not to reconcile.

- **Death:** The offender has died, but the hurt lingers.

- **Missing:** The offender has moved and cannot be located, so you can't have a conversation. Fortunately, with today's social media like LinkedIn and Facebook, it is easier to track people down.

- **Denial:** Refusal and rejection of the offender who says, "I didn't do anything wrong to hurt you!"

- **Desperate Fear:** You lack the skills, courage or motivation to ask for an apology. You avoid drama. "Are you kidding, I can't ask for an apology or forgiveness, that is impossible!"

- **Deciding Not to Let Go:** The un-forgiveness is on your part as you say, "I will never let go of what that person did to me."

Choose to Move to a Better Place: Reconciliation and Forgiveness

Reconciliation and forgiveness are healthy – for yourself and your relationships. Decide to "extend the olive branch" and make the first move. Seeking healing by asking for forgiveness is an act of the will, a choice.

Emotions may flow, but that is okay. Tears are not a sign of weakness; they are healing. If things get emotional, accept that. Your feelings are a normal part of the process. Don't wait until you "feel like it" to offer an apology. Do you only go out to feed the cows when you feel like it? Deal with the manure in your life that is keeping you down!

Alexander Chase said, "To understand is to forgive...even oneself."

All farmers, male and female, could benefit from great self-awareness. We all make choices. A woman at a farm crisis meeting once said, "Mom always told me that I had a choice in how to respond to what happened to me in my life. I could get bitter, or get better!"

You might want to ask a third party, a minister or counselor or facilitator to help you do a forgiveness ritual. This session can become a marker of "starting over" or "cleaning up the mess" to create a new chapter for your farm team. You identify the key issues that are keeping the family business stuck. You talk about what I call the bull in the middle of the room, the Undiscussabulls.

Focus on forgiveness, making repair and crafting a new code of conduct which aligns with your family business values and cherished beliefs.

Healing is the goal that will move your family and business forward.

Forgiveness is one of those "soft issues" farm families get frustrated with when they are "too frosted to forgive." Don't wait or procrastinate. The time to act is now. There's a multi-million-dollar farm waiting to grow, and rich legacy of relationship that needs to be re-established.

Remember, it is your farm, your family, and your choice. Make the choice today to mend the offenses and fences on your farm.

Notes:

_____

_____

_____

_____

_____

_____

_____

_____

_____

Chapter 8:

The Fine Art of Apologizing

Sometimes I wish I didn't have real-life examples of how I make mistakes, but my mishaps make good fodder for this book. Last harvest I was the combine driver who backed into the fuel truck while I was unloading my auger for cleanout to move to the next field. I have a bad habit of many accidents while backing up, so I should have checked my mirrors. The damage was a bent hydraulic shaft over the straw choppers, which was fixed with a $400 part, and no downtime, thankfully.

I told my husband that I was sorry for the mistake, and I thanked my son for quickly tracking down the part. Our employee also now understands the importance of not parking vehicles behind me.

Harvest this year is going to be extra fun because we all feel behind before we start due to the late season crops. I have already started praying for no frost until November! I'd like to share some practical ways to make things right that I learned from Gary Chapman and Jennifer Thomas this summer in their fabulous book called *When Sorry Isn't Enough*.

5 Ways to Say Sorry

1. "I'm Sorry"

You express regret. I was quick to do this after I heard the thud of hitting the truck. I also expressed regret to the semi-driver who grazed me as I was backing my SUV out of my garage onto my lane, rushing to get to the post office. I now always look down the lane before cranking out of the driveway! Sometimes expressing regret is all it takes to make restitution with the person you have offended, but recall the young kids who you've asked to say "sorry," and it comes out quickly from their little mouths, but with the wrong tone of voice, and no further change of behavior. Not a good thing.

2. "I Was Wrong"

Those folks who can accept responsibility for their hurtful actions get more traction with spouses who expect more than a quick sorry. This means that you accept the fact that you made a mistake and owned up to it. I was not going to sneak around the next field with a dented shaft; honesty is always the best policy in my books. Someone has torn a piece of sheet metal out of our shed, but we have never found anyone to own up to the mistake. Damage is done, but no one accepts responsibility. The hole is still not repaired!

3. "How Can I Make It Right?"

Making restitution. When I backed Wes's pickup into a car parked in my blind spot with the pickup hitch making a perfectly square hole in the car's front bumper, I was angry that the driver had not used his horn to stop me! I had to make it right with a $700 cheque to pay for a new car bumper, and I no longer drive the truck in town. Besides an apology, some people want to know what is going to change in the future with your actions so that you can make things right.

In harvest season when stress is high, you really need to focus on a positive attitude to catch people doing things right, so that you can build up the emotional bank account of all the harvesters. Be willing to take some difficult feedback if you are cutting too high, or the meals need to be timelier to the field. Don't take things personally, but seek out the ways other folks would like to be appreciated. Watch the tone of your voice on the FM radios. Long hours, dusty itchy backs, and poor yields make people cranky if you are not careful to check your attitude. Just making fresh hot coffee for my son and our employees "makes lots of things right" during busy field times. ·

4. "I Want to Change"

Genuinely repenting. In harvest season, you have habits around how you like to open up a field and the direction of the swaths. Sometimes getting folks to adopt a new way of doing things is stressful, until they can see the benefit. The swath driver needs to have some compassion for the grain cart guy or trucker as to the pattern created by the swaths. Are you open to the suggestion of changing your ways? Make a mind shift to be able to ask, "Is there something you would like me to do differently?"

5. "Can You Find it in Your Heart to Forgive Me?"

Requesting forgiveness takes courage, but the result is that you will feel better and lighter when you are forgiven. I appreciate having a spouse who doesn't yell or swear at me when I cause damage with backing up. He forgives me, and we move on. Chapman says that "for those with a controlling personality, asking forgiveness is out of their comfort zone emotionally. To successfully learn to speak the apology language of requesting forgiveness or, for that matter, any of the apology languages, an extremely controlling individual will likely require the help of a counselor or friend who is willing to be honest with him or her."

What Not to Say When Apologizing

So now you are primed for harvest, getting machines ready, and you've learned how to apologize in the right way. Here are Chapman's tips of what *not* to say when apologizing:

- Haven't you gotten over that yet?

- Why do you always...?

- What's the big deal?

- Give me a break.

- You just need to get over it.

- You sound like your mother

Try this instead:

- I did it, and I have no excuse.

- Can you ever forgive me?

- I realize that talk is cheap. I know that I need to show you how I will change.

- I will try to make this up to you by...

- You have every right to be upset.

I wish you all a very safe and successful harvest. In the sunny southwest of Manitoba, we have crops that are great, and in the terms of a teenager, some that suck! Take care of everyone on your team, and yourself with good sleep, great food, and gracious attitudes. I will do my best this year not to back into anything!

Notes:

_____

_____

_____

_____

_____

_____

_____

Chapter 9:

How to Deal with Bullying on the Farm

She came up to me quietly after my presentation, looking tired and sad. "Elaine, I haven't been off the farm in months, and I don't know who is going to help us with seeding. I am seventy, and I cannot take this anymore. My husband is very verbally abusive and won't get help for his depression. What do I do?"

This woman is a target of a bully according to the language of author Valerie Cade who wrote *Bully Free at Work – What You Can do to Stop Workplace Bullying Now!*

Bullying on farms is happening when targets are experiencing repeated disrespectful behavior. I can share many examples with you. The tactics according to Cade are exclusion, unreasonable demands, unfairness, verbal abuse and "crazy-making."

Can You Relate to These Farm Scenarios?

A **daughter-in-law** wonders how to get her name on the land titles after 25 years of marriage and years of working hard to make her father-in-law's farm succeed. Her husband is not willing to stand up for fairness and says nothing.

A **farm mom is not getting any support** to get treatment for her depressive husband, and she feels trapped. The exclusion from the community is killing her slowly.

A **wise widow who lives frugally** and wants to honor her husband's wishes is not sure why her adult children are making unreasonable demands for their inheritance. She is feeling threatened and pushed into making financial decisions that may leave her short of future family living funds. She has no idea what her long-term health care needs will be, and financial security is important to her, especially as she ages alone.

A **frustrated forty-year-old son** cannot get his father and mother to sign business agreements that share the farm assets and equity with the next generation. He is tired of the promise "just trust me" and wonders if other farmers work like slaves and get very low wages for years.

The over 60 father has no intention of retiring but knows that he likely needs to share the decision making with his successors. He is not happy about the barrage of verbal abuse he meets daily when he asks questions and tries to make a plan for the daily operations.

I need to stop. I could type pages of examples. I hear them frequently as a farm coach. My question is **"Why are you allowing the bad behavior to continue?"**

Valerie Cade outlines the experience of the workplace hosting bullies as one where "others say nothing, are not sure what to do or say. The bullying behavior is tolerated."

I say, "You get the behavior that you accept."

The bully minimizes the way the target feels and over time the farm team begins to think "This is just the way it is around here!" Bad behavior is ignored, and slowly the family (employees) become distant, silent, and non-creative according to Cade.

Targets of bullying suffer emotionally, physically, and spiritually. Cade's research finds that the target eventually quits (80 percent of the time). On farms, this gets very expensive with divorce and the loss of trained employees.

Are You Being Bullied?

Cade's book has some great tools, one of them being a self- assessment to help you determine if you are being bullied? To start, ask yourself the following questions:

Does the person you're having challenges with:

- Ignore you. Not return your phone calls or emails.

- Dismiss what you are saying or "put you down in the presence of others?"

- Spread rumors, lies, and half-truths about you?

- Routinely blame and criticize you?

There are many more questions too; for more, check out Cade's book.

What to Do About Bullies

Bullies cannot "flourish, or they cannot even survive in organizations committed to respect, open communication, and teamwork," says Cade.

In terms of dealing with bullies at the workplace, she suggests:

- Know your values and communicate them.

- Use managers as role models.

- Develop more open communication.

- Provide a complaint process.

- Train people about bullying.

- Support interpersonal skills training and conflict resolution.

- Punish bullies.

- Don't hire bullies.

- Adopt an anti-bullying policy.

14 Ways to Make Your Farm Bully-Free

The subject of bullying was also a chapter in my own book *Farming's In-Law Factor*. Co-author Dr. Megan McKenzie and I came up with a list of ways to address the nastiness you might be experiencing on your farm.

1. Accept that there are various reasons that people are nasty, some of which we will never know or understand. You can accept the reality of the nastiness, but you do not have to accept bad bullying behavior.

2. Be curious, not judgmental. Address the root cause of the nastiness (e.g., depression, trauma, health issues).

3. Think of a positive trait that you can acknowledge them for.

4. Name the behavior as nasty or inappropriate. Some people don't realize they are being donkeys.

5. Pray or reflect on a new approach or perspective to engage the person.

6. Do not accept guilt or shame.

7. Create physical or emotional space from the nastiness.

8. Set healthy boundaries.

9. Make requests. For example, if you feel you are being excluded, make a request. For example, "I would like to be included in the emails to be part of the farm meetings."

10. Write a heartfelt letter and deliver it. Or burn it. Just putting your feelings on paper can help ease the hurt.

11. Give the person an undeserved act of grace. Cade suggests responding with "I understand. I see."

12. Choose not to be melodramatic about the nastiness or take it personally. Cade coach's folks to move to the "I am being bullied, and I will now take steps to protect myself" stage. "Notice if you are feeling angry, frustrated or hurt. It is time to channel these

feelings, so they do not take a toll on your body, mind, and well-being."

13. Resist the urge to criticize, as it can become a bad habit.

14. Realize that some people act grumpy or mean (almost as performance art in some cases) in order to get attention or because they have come to believe that is who they are.

Together you and your farm team can work towards a bully free farm culture.

Notes:

_____

_____

_____

_____

_____

_____

_____

_____

_____

_____

Chapter 10:

Communication Essentials: Making Your Voice Heard on the Farm

In Hershey, Pennsylvania, I gave a presentation on "Conflict Dynamics in Family Business" to vegetable and fruit growers. The thread of conversation that struck me was from the non-family members (i.e., employees) who were looking for ways to have a voice in the decision-making of the farm. This hits home for me, as we have two non-family employees on our farm. Do they feel like their opinion counts? How do we find out?

Here are seven tips to help non-family members learn how to use their voice to help in the family farm decision process.

How to Make Your Voice Heard on the Farm

Use Your Voice

First comes the decision to actually speak up. When doing so, be gracious and respectful. Come from curiosity. "I was wondering if you would be open to me giving you some input on this problem we are trying to solve." I cannot read minds. I need to hear your voice and your opinion. Be silent no longer.

Try to Understand the Perspectives

Try to understand the perspectives of the owners and shareholders of the farm. Managers are juggling many priorities. Make sure your timing for your request is reasonable. It really helps if the farm team has a formalized process like a staff meeting with a clear agenda. This gives you time to prepare your approach, do your research, and process how you would like to express yourself.

Stop Yielding

Yielding is a negative conflict resolution tool if you are always giving in to the other partners or employees. Your opinion and ideas count. A seasoned farm woman confessed to me that her throat actually closed up when she was getting ready to make a strong statement to her farming brother and father. Her lack of validation over the years had created a physical habit of constricting her voice. She discovered this tendency when she was working with a therapeutic massage specialist.

Take Baby Steps to Build Up Your Confidence

Perhaps the first approach is to write down your ideas on paper, in a Word document, or use a mind mapping technique to branch out all of your ideas. If you are nervous in communicating, you can use the notes as your talking script. I have seen this be very effective with a sensitive widow who wanted to communicate clearly her estate planning intentions with her distraught adult children.

Read Conversational Intelligence: How Great Leaders Build Trust and Get Extraordinary Results by Judith E. Glaser

In *Conversational Intelligence: How Great Leaders Build Trust and Get Extraordinary Results*, Glaser speaks of Level 3, or transformational, conversations that build trust, are transparent and build a relationship. She says "unhealthy conversations are at the root of distrust, deceit, betrayal and avoidance...which leads to lower productivity and innovation, and ultimately lower success. "

Build Your Star Skills™

In the same book mentioned above, Glaser suggests using skills that achieve results, including building report, listening without judgment, asking discovery questions, reinforcing success, and dramatizing the message. In other words, let every voice on your farm team be heard. Choose your words of encouragement carefully to build rapport. Learn from one another with a learner mindset, not judging, and celebrate the wins! You need to let people challenge new ideas before they can accept them.

Love Does Not Read Minds

No more silence at the farm board meeting table. Give everyone a chance to express their thoughts openly and without fear. Seek to understand the other person's intent, their "why." Let people have time to tell stories to get their points across. Fear shuts out people's voices. Create a place where honesty, empathy, and a shared vision of success for the farm is welcomed. Use great listening skills and discovery questions to build understanding. Your goal is to increase the transparency of your conversations in your farm business and your family.

Create a Vision Board for Your Farm

Cut out pictures of what success for your farm looks like or print them off your phone or Instagram collage.

Glaser says that "as you learn how to create more space for trust to grow, you change the conversational landscape." Vision boards are just another way to communicate what reality you are aiming for on your farm. Perhaps the word TRUST needs to be on your board.

"If you want to build a ship, don't drum up people together to collect wood, and don't assign them tasks and work, but rather teach them to long for the endless immensity of the sea." – Antoine De Saint-Exupery

If you are longing to have more of a voice on your farm because you can see the immense potential ahead, it is time to speak up, speak out, and be heard.

Notes:

_____

_____

_____

_____

_____

_____

_____

_____

_____

Chapter 11:

Handling Interpersonal Conflict

You are likely exhausted from harvest as you have grabbed this book for a few moments of "down time." Harvest stress gives everyone on the farm team a chance to show their true colors, including how they manage mistakes and high tension.

My question for you is, are you tired of the conflict avoidance dance on your farm? Are you finally ready to prevent destructive conflict avoidance?

5 Tips for Dealing with Interpersonal Conflict

I bet there are folks on your farm who are ready to work out issues, yet they are highly frustrated by those who usually avoid conflict. They often tell me, "I can't deal with someone who won't talk to me and tell me what the problem is!" So how can you deal with the "strong silent types" who won't engage with you?

Here are some tips from William Wilmot and Joyce Hocker, authors of *Interpersonal Conflict*.

1. Put Them at Ease

Use a non-threatening approach—calm voice, friendly and open non-verbal actions (like extending your hand when you are asking someone to dance). Don't trap them in the pick-up or a small space, and consider sharing a meal together to talk things over. Breaking bread together has a huge impact on setting a good tone for a tough conversation. Pie makes people happy, I am told!

2. Provide Safety

Set ground rules ("I promise I won't raise my voice or interrupt you") and let them have time to prepare for the discussion. I usually ask "Is this a good time for us to talk? If not, when would work better?"

3. Change the Mode of Communication

Please don't text! If you have been using emails, talk face to face; try writing out a letter if talking in person doesn't work. I have seen the power of the written word with a young successor who carefully laid out his vision for the farm on paper, and then shared it with his parents. He typed it on the computer so that he could correct the tone of his letter. He was also careful to thank his parents for the opportunities they had provided, and he made requests in a polite manner.

4. Frame the Conversation as Relationship-Building

You might say "I have a suggestion for how you could help build our relationship." Or "Our project needs some help. Would you be able to talk with me about our timeline?"

5. Do Not Say "We Need to Talk"

That strikes fear into the heart of most folks.

How to Deal with Your Own Conflict Avoidance

According to Wilmot and Hocker, "If you see yourself as an avoider, we hope you will want to expand your repertoire to be able to collaborate, confront, stay engaged, and even escalate when needed. You will need to find the sources of your fearful responses, be willing to take breaks when you need to, practice initiating important conversations instead of waiting for others to initiate (this gives you a sense of necessary control), and focus on what is actually happening in the interaction instead of only how you feel."

If you're feeling overwhelmed by conflict, you may need to ask a third party for help in resolving the conflict. That is why I will never be out of a job as a farm family coach. Farm families are entangled in the avoidance dance, and they want it to stop.

If you keep avoiding conflict, others around you will avoid all hot issues to take care of you, but I can tell you right now, they are sick and tired of walking on eggshells on your farm.

Their other options are to get really mad, which is called escalating, or threaten to leave. Either of these dances sets in motion a destructive system. "You may see yourself as the victim, or as the one who is right but persecuted," says Wilmot. He says you can change your sense of self by adopting new, risky, but rewarding conflict skills.

Here are his tips for working with your own avoidance:

Safety Comes First

If you do not feel protected, you can't use productive conflict skills. If your partner shows any history or signs of physically harming you, work only with a third party. If you own a grain bagger, be careful. I have seen this machine cause father and son come to fisticuffs on more than one occasion!

Take Breaks If You Freeze When You Are Afraid

Let others know what is going on, "This is hard for me, I need to take a break, but I will be back." You won't be seen as an avoider but as a careful person. In mediation, we call these "caucus" breaks where the person speaks privately to the mediator to get their bearings and more understanding or information.

Ask for the Dance

Learn to initiate conversations rather than waiting. John Gottman calls this "making quick repair." Don't let issues fester and boil. Engage!

Ask for Help If You Are Stuck

The greatest gift we can give each other is the sense of being heard. Talk to a professional third party, the farm stress line counselor, or a trusted friend to work out how you want to address your conflict situation. I have many resources on my website to encourage better conflict resolution.

Notes:

_____

_____

_____

_____

_____

_____

_____

_____

_____

_____

TEAMS & OPERATIONS

Chapter 12:

How to Avoid Under Appreciation by Tracking Farm Work Loads

"You don't know what you've got til' it's gone..." is the line in a song that may ring true for families who regret not paying attention to earlier cries for understanding. My co-writer Dr. Megan McKenzie has a few thoughts about the importance of tracking where time on the farm is spent:

There seem to be several themes in farm families that are struggling. One theme is that farm families that are in conflict often don't appreciate their in-laws or what their in-laws are contributing to their family and their farm until after the in-laws have had enough and jumped ship. In the course of our busy lives, it is simple to overlook all the work that others in our lives do, particularly if we don't have the warmest feelings towards them in the first place. It's easy to take people for granted. Whether it's a brother-in-law (BIL) that spends hours keeping old machinery running or a mother-in-law (MIL) that fixes meals and runs errands, these acts can just blur into the scenery, especially if they occur regularly or have happened for long periods of time.

Unappreciated Work on the Farm

I'd like to start out with a story that serves as an example of how sometimes work can go unappreciated on the farm. The scenario has played out again and again across the country with only slight variations on the theme. Here is one version that may seem very familiar to you.

The daughter-in-law (DIL) moved into her husband's family's century-old farm house. She worked off the farm at a full-time job while raising kids, making meals, and fixing up the old house. She mowed the lawn and kept the flower beds. She helped with chores in the barn year-round and drove equipment in the field in summer. Like many DILs, she learned to do the farm bookkeeping. She helped feed the family with her garden, eggs, chickens, and fall preserving.

Yet, she was never appreciated. So, she worked harder, hoping to be acknowledged for efforts. Her kids grew up, and she grew tired of the mistreatment and continual barrage of abusive words about her shortcomings. All attempts to work out a solution failed, and she finally left the farm. To replace her labor, the farm had to hire five staff people (a combination of seasonal, full-time, and contract) to cover all the tasks she had been doing, and there were still gaps that had to be filled by her husband or that were left uncompleted.

How to Prevent Under Appreciation with Time Logs

We need to make a conscious effort to think about all of the things that the people around us do that contribute to our lives, to our family, and to our farm. It will help us to be a bit more appreciative and a bit more empathetic when they forget something or make one those mistakes that are oh so human.   One of the ways to do that is to have all the members of the family document how they spend their time for one week.

This will help us to recognize the efforts that may go unnoticed and often unappreciated. In some families, it may highlight a discrepancy between workloads and compensation. In other families, a time log, alongside a list of what the family members say they value, may show whether they are on the road they want to be on. For some family members, the time log may show workaholic tendencies or attempts to avoid other aspects of their lives. It may help us learn things about our in-laws that we didn't know. It is important that family members be honest as bluffing only defeats the purpose.

Use the following chart to reflect and log your daily activities. Have your farm team fill out their own logs too. Then make copies for everyone and come together in a family business meeting to discuss.

Time Log: How My Time Is Spent on the Farm

Time	Monday	Tuesday	Wednesday	Thursday	Friday	Saturday	Sunday
7AM	Eat		Run				Sleep
8AM	Chores						
ETC.							

Time Log Reflection Questions

After the time logs are filled out, it's time to review your log and the logs of your farm team. Here are some questions to reflect upon.

Individual Reflection

What are your first thoughts when you read over your own time log?

Does anything on your own time log surprise you?

If you could change anything about how you spend your time, what would that be?

How do you feel about your own work on the farm?

Farm Team Reflection

What are your first thoughts when you see others' time logs?

How do you feel about how the workload is being distributed among team members?

How do you feel about how people are being compensated for labor on the farm?

How do roles and responsibilities need to change?

On a scale of 1 to 10, with 10 being great, how happy are the farm team players with their workload on the farm?

Time Logs: An Important Lesson

Feeling unappreciated for the work done on the farm is unfortunately common. Here is another story to think about.

It was very important to the brother-in-law that he would have time with his young family. However, between his full-time off-farm job in the city and spending almost every evening fixing machinery on the farm, he hardly ever saw his kids. He was expected to do on-farm work but was seldom acknowledged for it. He received little compensation in terms of money or assets, yet was considered lazy or a bad family member if he didn't keep giving freely of his time.

How he was spending his time didn't reflect his values. His wife was tired of essentially being a single parent, and it was straining their marriage, yet he was struggling to start the discussion to get out of this predicament because of family pressure.

Perhaps if the brother-in-law kept a time log for a week, he would have hard evidence of how he typically spends his time. The couple could use facts to back up their story and talk about solutions with the extended family.

Unfortunately, many farm families that I have coached refuse to do this exercise. You likely will not change what you have not measured. Get started by filling out your time log today, and let me know how time tracking works for your farm team.

Notes:

Chapter 13:

Farm Mentoring: Why, How, and Guiding Principles for Success

Things on our farm are changing again, an employee moving on. In Stephen Poulter's book, *The Father Factor*, he talks about the fathering style of a "compassionate mentor." This is a great style for farm founders to embrace over the winter months as they train the next generation for success. Smart farm dads and moms realize that family employees who stay farming are happy and passionate about their farm team roles.

6 Reasons We Need Compassionate Mentors on the Farm

Let's look at some of the reasons why we need more merciful mentors on our farms.

1. Successful people have great role models and people who share wisdom. This is true in any career, including farming.

2. We need different people at different stages of our life. Our young married son has a great connection with peer farmers, but he also relies on input from his father who has over 35 years' experience in the game of farming.

3. "The Lone Ranger" is a myth, says Rev. Gaetane Marshall. She says that we need a support system to survive, one with accountability checks. Do you know any "Lone Ranger" farmers who refuse to ask for help from professional advisors?

4. Affirmation is necessary for survival. A letter of appreciation and encouragement to your farming son/daughter or parents this Christmas is probably the most priceless gift that you can give. Put pen to paper, or keyboard to printer, and share affirmations with your farm team, especially your family.

5. We need someone to show us how it is done. And be flexible to do it in a new way.
New technology is not "new" to someone who has never known any different, i.e. our young successor son. He keeps telling me just to keep pushing buttons because he knows I am afraid something will break, which of course it will not!

6. Mentoring is your opportunity to "pass on the baton" as John Maxwell says. It creates legacy.

Finding the Right Mindset for Mentoring

"Mentoring is investing in the life of another person, a service of increasing someone else to make them great, decreasing self and releasing the gifts of another," says Gaetane Marshall.

As a farm family coach, it brings me huge joy to hear a farming dad say "Elaine, I made a lot of mistakes in my early years, which I really want to protect my son from repeating." This is the heart's cry of a successful business person being very self-aware of how his actions impact the learning points of his successor. This father has an attitude of lifelong learning and wisdom to empower the next generation with. He is not interested in being controlling, cloning himself, criticizing or making himself co-dependent with the next generation. As mentors, we all need to be wise about setting boundaries, and not doing too much for one we are mentoring.

How attractive are you as a mentor? Do you manage your emotions well? Can you see difficult feedback as a learning and growth opportunity rather than judgment?

Attitude is a huge deal. Watching a father and son discuss options for capital purchases, marketing, and production with a respectful tone and sense of "equality as partners" is a beautiful thing. Getting calls about the founders who refuse to make new shareholder agreements or come to a table for open discussion of a new vision for the farm is depressing.

Mentoring in Motion: How Mentoring Works

There is an expectation of an exchange of ideas with respect and accountability when the mentoring relationship is working well.

Here is Marshall's list (farmers love concise lists I am told) of mentoring in motion:

1. Assess.

2. Watch for potential, passion and positive attitude.

3. Initiate and invest. Set boundaries, don't over-function.

4. Give timely advice.

5. Be a role model. (Handle communication and conflict well!)

6. Give encouragement, feedback, correction, accountability, discipline.

7. Provide co-working training opportunities.

8. Give freedom, to make mistakes and adopt a learning culture.

9. Expect a good return and exchange of ideas and outcomes.

10. Follow-up. What is working well? What is not working so great?

7 Principles to Guide Mentoring Relationships

As a Christian, Rev. Gaetane Marshall sees mentoring principles from the wisdom of Biblical principles. Use these thoughts for insight on how you want to show up in your farm or business as a compassionate mentor. People of principle and integrity make fantastic mentors.

The Barnabus Principle

It's not about you. You must decrease so another may increase and so God can release.

Free Will and Follow Principle

They choose to follow or not. This is not about coercing your successor to be mentored by you.

The Principle of Exchange

It is a relationship of living, giving exchange. Both bring something to the relationship. Many sons would just love their dad/bosses to say "I am proud of you and all that you accomplished here this year!"

The Elijah and Elisha Principle

The principle of the double portion. Elisha had a servant's heart, increasing Elijah's spiritual inheritance. Some farming sons will surpass the growth of the founders, increasing the value of the farm business. Can everyone celebrate this success?

The Principle of a Transitioning Figure

Rather than a permanent fixture. Mentors are in our lives for a time, and a season, they are not meant to be "forever" as at some stage the relationship becomes one of "co-mentoring" each other.

The Principle of Transparency

We are all human, and we all make mistakes. Compassionate mentors can share failures and successes.

The Principle of Sowing and Reaping

This principle is hard-wired into farmers who expect a harvest. What you reap, you will sow, so sow generously.

Notes:

_____

_____

_____

_____

_____

_____

_____

_____

_____

_____

Chapter 14:

Women on the Farm:
The Importance of Assessing Roles

In May we celebrate Mother's Day, but I think we should be celebrating the many roles of farm women every day of the year. We can do this by "checking in" to see what is still a good role for mom and what she would like to let go of.

For some farm women who are following the rules of "you should do this, we always have done that," there is a burden of expectation that she would like to shed.

The reality is that on many family farms, traditional western gender roles still play out. Mother-in-laws (MILs) and daughter-in-laws (DILs) often find themselves working closely together with each other and with the other women in the family. The harmony in the farm team unit will likely increase if folks are honest with each other about which roles are still ones they want to embrace, and which tasks they would rather not do.

Assessing Roles on the Farm

For this exercise, brainstorm a list of roles taken on by the MIL, DIL, or other women in the family. We have created a form for you to fill out, but feel free to add additional roles that are important on your farm.

Beside each role, record who does this task and whether this is working for each person involved. If any of the tasks that have been assigned, delegated, or dropped-on-lap are not working for one or more party, discuss possible solutions to the problem.

- Maybe there is someone else on the farm team that would be better suited to that role?

- Perhaps the duties could be shared, thus lightening each person's burden?

- Is it possible that the roles is not working because she needs acknowledgment for the work that she is doing?

Balancing out the workload may mean swapping tasks, reducing the number of tasks, hiring or recruiting extra help, or agreeing to reduce expectations around tasks. Sometimes these trade-offs make a world of difference for those involved, even though they can sometimes be hard to swallow. Some examples include: when the women are helping to combine, the men also help make meals; hiring a part-time bookkeeper; reducing the size of the garden; putting young children in daycare, or seeking out government homecare to help care for aging relatives.

Notes:

_____

_____

_____

_____

_____

_____

_____

_____

_____

Worksheet: Assessing Roles on the Farm

Role	MIL Does this task – this is working for her	DIL Does this task – this is not working for her	Other: Name Does not do this task
Making/Taking Meals to Field			
Keeping Farm Records			
Caring for Children or Aging Family Members			
Running for Parts			
Working at an off Farm Job			
Spending Time with Family			
Resolving Conflicts			
Getting Input from Non-Farm Family Members			
Arranging the Social Calendar & Family Appointments			
Serving as the Family Social Worker			
Bookkeeping			

Worksheet: Assessing Roles on the Farm

Role	MIL	DiL	Other: Name
	Does this task – this is working for her	Does this task – this is not working for her	Does not do this task
Gardening			
Maintaining Yard and House			
Making/Taking Meals to Field			
Acting as Extra Hands as Needed			

Chapter 15:

3 Questions to Improve the Decision-Making Process on the Farm

One of speaker Norm Rubin's universal laws of life goes like this: "Make everyone a stakeholder. Involve everyone on your team in your farm; ask for their input and opinions. Recognize that all those involved in your business will build your business. When you make everyone in your network a stakeholder, whether they have a financial or emotional investment in your business, then they will produce like they have never produced before."

Do you agree with Rubin?

Making decisions on the family farm can be emotional and frustrating if the decision-making style is one of "benevolent dictatorship" – this style of listening to Dad's direction because it is "his way or the highway" kind of thinking. These farms do not have an inclusive model of decision making that listens to or respects all the team's inputs.

Remember you have two systems in play here: the family dynamic and the farm business system. Here are some helpful overview questions to help the decision-making process from NDSU Fargo's Sean Brotherson.

3 Questions to Improve the Decision-Making Processes on Your Farm

1. What Is the Issue or Concern That We Need to Make a Decision About?

The father is typically keyed into operational decisions to keep the farm production high and profitable. The successor is thinking a bit more on the strategic side and wondering, *"When do I get to be the manager and have ultimate control of the final decisions on this farm?"* Mom is trying hard to separate the family issues from the business concerns, but she seems to get caught in the cross-fire of angst from her husband and her adult son. Her key decision is to have a process or place to sit down to talk things through and get some action on making a decision for change! The daughter-in-law is busy with her off-farm job and wonders when she will be able to contribute her perspectives in the decision-making process. She feels her voice doesn't count because no one asks for her opinions.

Whether it is operational decisions, financial decisions, or something else, the first step is identifying where decision-making must take place and who wants to be part of the conversation.

2. What Are the Values That Will Guide Us in Setting Goals Related to Work and Our Family?

Values are the cherished beliefs that we hold. I have a values assessment tool that indicates my top 7 values as spirituality, intimacy, honesty, challenge, friendship, independence, and accomplishment. These are the drivers for the work that gives me meaning and purpose. When a farm family team has conflicting values, no amount of talking is going to fix things! As Brotherson states, "Families tend to be more happy and successful when they have shared values and goals."

Here is an example of how different values can cause strain on the farm: If Dad is blind to the need to build relationship with time off for fun and family (values held by other farm team members), he will continue to demand 100-hour work weeks and drive away the desire of the next generation to copy his work style.

I agree with Brotherson, "The decisions we make, the way we use our time, and the things we spend money on are influenced by the values we have." What are your top 7 values? Compare your list to your spouse and your farm team members. What is negotiable for you and what is non-negotiable? What values are guiding the decisions made on your farm?

3. What Are the Costs and Benefits of the Decision?

"Costs refer to a decrease in what a person values, such as less autonomy or economic security. Benefits refer to an increase in those things that are valued, such as increased time together or better personal esteem," says Brotherson.

Consider at what point the costs are going to outweigh the benefits of a certain decision. For example, working off-farm helps the cash flow, but the cost of vehicles, food, child care, clothing, processed meals, etc. may not be worth it. Women who work off-farm may be doing it more for personal satisfaction than economic gain. Both costs and benefits must be weighed when making the decision.

Different families have different styles of decision making. Some autonomous folks may rest the ultimate decision with one family member, usually, the one most affected by the decision. Other families have a more collaborative style whereby making the decision is shared jointly via consensus. On highly stressed farms, the style for decisions tends to rest with the founder, usually the father or husband who is dominant in decision making.

I hope you'll do some work on identifying your top 7 key values. I encourage you to challenge the decision-making habits that may not be working for you and engage a new approach. Also, remember that procrastination in not making a decision to act is indeed a decision.

Notes:

_____

_____

_____

_____

_____

_____

_____

_____

_____

_____

Chapter 16:

What Does Caring for the Farm Look Like?

I've just read David Specht's book *The Farm Whisperer: Secrets to Preserving Families and Perpetuating Farms*. It's a great, quick read of inspiring questions for farm families wanting to transition management and ownership to create a successful legacy. Specht and I met on the Internet...I Googled him, then picked up the phone, and we exchanged books. Don't worry; we are both happily married. We both are passionate about families and farms having a great future.

Specht has created an app called "Inspired Questions for Farmers," and the one question that caught my attention was this one:

Does Anyone Care About the Farm as Much as I Do?

What is your answer?

Dad

Founder with aching back, more wrinkles, and a deep sense of responsibility to make sure all the high priority tasks are completed on a timely basis. Dad, are you asking great questions to the successor that you are intentionally grooming? Did you seek out his or her perspective on what the priorities for the day were? What does "lack of caring" actually look like to you? Is it the sloppy job done when cleaning out the bin, the barn, or the shop? Is it leaving early to go home to read bedtime stories to toddlers? Is it choosing to spend time with friends hitting a few targets after your team has already logged a 100-hour work week? Don't stew about the "lack of care scenarios" in your head Dad. We cannot read you mind. You have to tell us what is frustrating you!

If you are consumed by the work of the farm, dad, as you have few friends and no hobbies, then it may be time for a new perspective.

Yes, the grass needs to be cut, but perfection is not everyone's standard, and maybe cutting the grass every three days is excessive, not just a message that you care lots about how the farm looks and others are busy doing other tasks.

Mom

Because you care about the farm, you are willing to do night checks during calving, bathe calves in warm water, and bottle-feed newborn livestock. You use your nurturing skills for your children and your farm animals. You show care in many ways, but you too are noticing that your energy levels are decreased significantly by 8 pm. You would really like to delegate some of your jobs to the next generation, but have a hard time asking for what you need. You don't want to appear weak or needy.

Today, I am giving you permission to say these words:

- ☐ "I think that we all should talk about what the farm priorities are for the next three months."

- ☐ "I need to have some help with my jobs, and share the load, as I am losing energy these days."

- ☐ "I sometimes feel that no one else on this farm team cares about the farm as much as I do."

- ☐ "I want us to sit down and discuss openly our needs, feelings and wants for the future vision of this amazing farm operation. I also want more time for fun and family. "

Successor

Do you care about the farm as much as your parents? What are things you currently do to show the founders how much you appreciate the roles and responsibilities you fulfill on the farm? Do you communicate to your parents with compassion when they seem to be losing some of their resilience, especially during stressful times? When you suggest changes in roles or behavior to make things easier or to try a new project for growth are you met with collaborative communication and good decision making? What does really caring for the well-being and success of the farm look like to you in practical terms?

Spouse

You have a voice, too. Are you able to voice your observations as the one with "fresh eyes" from your family of origin experiences? Do you feel respected for your role in providing off-farm income to the farm's cash flow and your family's needs? Does caring for the farm for you come in the form of contributing labor to the farm when you can, but ultimately saving your energy and efforts for the off-farm job and child care?

Everyone

Have a meeting and talk about what "caring for the farm" means to you, and in practical terms, how it can be acted out.

- ## Financial Care

Accounts are kept up to date, bills are paid, books are entered currently, and the financial analysis is shared with the farm team. Contingency plans are in place, and the team of advisors for tax, investments, and debt servicing are all on board with the farm's business plan, succession plan, and estate plan.

- ## Operational Care

The equipment is well-maintained in a decently organized shop. People are keen to clean up their messes and put tools back where they belong. Everyone treats equipment well and observes safe handling habits. Landlord relations are great, and production plans are in place to help the next generation have some ownership. Buildings are well-maintained, and the yard looks well-kept.

- ## Emotional Care

It is okay to ask for what you need. Conflicts are embraced when there is a difference in perspective for solving problems. Emotions are not hidden but expressed with respect and patience. People adapt by reading the behavior and language of others because they truly care that the farm team has a great culture to work in.

- ## Physical Care

Farmers are aging. We all are. Our bodies need good self-care in order to be able to make the long journey of the seasons of farming. Mental health asks for times of renewal and refreshing which can happen in short breaks during the work day and scheduled holiday time. Is it time to have a visit with your doctor?

Caring for the farm shows up for different folks in different ways. Give everyone permission to describe what their picture of "caring for the farm" looks like. Celebrate the good. Make some changes to transform the "not so good."

Notes:

_____

_____

_____

_____

_____

_____

_____

_____

_____

PLANNING

Chapter 17:

Setting Goals: The Year-In-Review Questionnaire

When a new year arrives, it is important to reflect upon the previous year and make pans for the upcoming year. Take down last year's calendar, review your diary, and give yourself a moment to reflect on how the year went and what you want to achieve this year. To help you out I've created a Year in Review tool. Grab your pen and fill out the form below.

Year-In-Review Questionnaire

1. What do I remember and value from the past year?

2. Your accomplishments:

3. Your disappointments:

4. What did you learn this past year?

5. I learned from what I did accomplish that...

6. I learned from what I did not accomplish that...

7. If I reframe my learnings into counsel for the coming year, I hear myself advising...

8. What did the past year teach you about how you should approach the coming year differently?

9. I notice that I experience a definite resistance (pushback) that limits either my accomplishments or my being who I most genuinely am. This resistance looks and feels like... (note – I call these "boulders." Understanding them will help you push through)

10. The eight most deeply held beliefs or core values that I want to live by in the next year are...

Value 1:

Value 2:

Value 3:

Value 4:

Value 5:

Value 6:

Value 7:

Value 8:

11. What are at least two goals for each of the roles I will have in the next year?

Personal (physical, mental, emotional & spiritual well-being and growth)

Goal 1:

Goal 2:

Family (marriage/partners, children)

Goal 1:

Goal 2:

Friends

Goal 1:

Goal 2:

Work

Goal 1:

Goal 2:

Neighborhood/Community

Goal 1:

Goal 2:

My World

Goal 1:

Goal 2:

12. Out of all the goals listed, what are my top 5 goals for next year?

Top Goal #1:

Top Goal #2:

Top Goal #3:

Top Goal #4:

Top Goal #5:

13. Who am I willing to share this with in order to be accountable and responsible for achieving these goals? How can I also keep track of my own progress and motivate myself to achieve these goals?

Congratulate Yourself for Your Thoughtful Work

There is power in your pencil and pen. I know that many of the "next gen" use thumbs instead of pencils, but whatever works, use it. Studies have shown that folks who write their thoughts out in journals live longer. There is also research that shows those who commit goals to paper or computer are more likely to hit the marks and targets they set.

Many farm families tell me that they just want "a happy family;" they want harmony and time to hang out together as a family. Okay, what does that look like in practice? If that is your goal, perhaps you could set some weekends aside now for fun at the lake, either in the snow, or in the summer with the boat, canoe, kayak, or wiener sticks!

Or if you have goals to build neighborhood and community relationships, decide who is hosting the next gathering and block out the dates early. We all lead very "busy" full lives, but we all make choices to commit to what is really important.

My goal for this year is to continue to cherish family and relationships since intimacy and friendship are two of my top six values. I know this to be true as I have a Value Styles Indicator assessment that I use with myself and my farm family clients. If you would like more clarity about the different beliefs or common values that are driving your farm team, contact me, and I'll set up the assessment for your farm team online. Conflict is fueled when the values you embrace are not honored in your farm workplace. Perhaps the tension triggers you are experiencing are a result of messed up or incongruent value expectations.

Make sure that your goals align with what you truly value and cherish, then your chances of success in hitting your targets and achieving your goals will be greatly enhanced.

Notes:

Chapter 18:

Identifying and Accomplishing Goals and Priorities

"Hey, watch out, there's a rock the size of a loaf of bread about to go through the header!!" I yell to my new hubby in the cab of our combine as we harvest in 1981.

"Don't worry, I saw it, and there will be more." he confides to me.

As a Red River Valley farm girl transported by marriage to the Waskada Clay Loam of Southwestern Manitoba, I have developed the habit of picking stones or rocks on my field walks as I deliver meals, fuel, or help out with the harvest. I wasn't used to picking rocks in my childhood near Dugald because there weren't any.

Time to Go Rock Picking

January is a great time for rock picking on your farms, but these rocks are not in your fields, they are in your heads. They are the priorities – what the late Stephen R. Covey, author of *Seven Habits for Highly Effective People*, calls the "big rocks." They are the things you need to put into your jar of life first, in order to get them accomplished, then the pebbles, sand and other demands on your time will fill up your life's time container. If you don't put the big rocks in first, the daily interruptions, breakdowns, and distractions (pebbles and sand) will pull you off the path you thought your farm and family were trekking down. Your time jar will be full, but you won't be happy because the big rocks did not get accomplished.

Recently in a farm family meeting with mom, dad, four adult children workers (the successors) and one spouse, we had an "ah ha" moment. The oldest worker and successor had ten years of working alongside Dad and Mom, and he was very confident in what he could accomplish in a day. His three siblings were struggling to catch up to the oldest sibling's sense of confidence. One brave soul confronted Dad at the meeting with a plea to not be too eager to let go of leadership and management of the farm too quickly but to have a mentorship and learning plan so that she could capture the skills and capacity to do awesome, efficient work in her roles on the farm. Each adult worker and successor was asking for better communication and a clearer direction of the tasks and skills required for each day. Dad was coached to concentrate on having a mentor/leadership role to train the next generation fully before letting go of his "ultimate decision maker" role.

But how were they going to accomplish this on a practical basis?

Block the Calendar

I walked over to the large year calendar on the farm office wall. It was blank. The dates and months were there of course, but nothing was written on it. That is changing for 2016. Each month is going to be blocked with the tasks, jobs, and priorities; the BIG ROCKS that the team needs to address. The main manager, Dad, is going to document daily in his field notes on his phone what he is doing and what needs to be prepared for. It will become a living document of the jobs, priorities, and timelines that need to be honored for their specialized farm. The field notes are accessible on the main office computer for all workers to monitor.

Ranking Goals and Priorities

I have seen the same plea from another family where the office manager did not have a clear sense of the patterns of management for the seasons of the year. She·just wanted Dad to write down the monthly priorities and goals so she could get a sense of what needed to be done, and what was a lesser demand on her time.

Michael Pantalon's book, *Instant Influence: How to Get Anyone to Do Anything*, has six helpful questions in getting people to understand what is important to accomplish. He uses a range of one to ten, with ten being most important to help folks get a clear quantitative feedback.

For instance, on a scale of 1 to 10, how important is it that we get this job done this week? If the manager says 9, then you know what the big rock is for the week. If he says 2, then other jobs take higher priority. You could also use this ranking system for the agenda items proposed for your operational meetings.

Communication Differences

Some women have the tendency to use "rapport" as the way they prefer to communicate which drives some men crazy according to Deborah Tannen who wrote, *You Just Don't Understand: Women and Men in Conversation.* Men prefer to have a concise "report," just the facts, please. So, there needs to be some compromise in understanding different communication styles as folks talk about the priorities of the farm and decide on the size of the rock that needs to be picked.

Where Time Is Spent

Another issue in priority setting is getting a clearer picture of where time is spent. My farm clients who love their smartphones are using a program called Exaktime to track the work hours and what duties are being accomplished. Again, this tool helps with reporting the facts, the jobs done, and how much time they took.

If the work ethic of two siblings is different, the time tracking program on their phones will account for the actual hours spent working. To be paid, they have to submit the Exact time records. The time sheets for the entire work crew are available on the office computer, and records of the jobs accomplished are shared at the weekly meetings.

Someone once said, "You can only change what you can measure." Farm conflicts about who is working harder and longer hours is not uncommon. Perhaps it is time to invest in a tool to track what is actually getting done, by whom. You can start to monitor who is a good rock picker and who is fooling around in the sand or throwing pebbles, but not making the "main thing the main thing," to quote Stephen Covey.

When I go for walks along the field roads, I also like to find flat rocks to make inspiration plaques for young girls I mentor. I can write words to encourage them, and the rocks are a reminder to them that I value their growth as young women. I won't find too many of these treasures in January, so it takes planning to harvest the rocks I need in the right season. Remember, planning ahead is a good thing. Block out the big rock activities on your yearly calendar. Think about using color coding for each worker. Do whatever works for your style and system, but do it!

Notes:

_____

_____

_____

_____

_____

_____

_____

_____

_____

Chapter 19:

Planning and Decluttering for Your Move Off the Farm

The number 2020 stares at me from the flipchart paper on my kitchen wall. This farm coach is being coached to set timelines for moving off our farm yard to make room for our successor to live in the main yard. I have four harvests left to get things checked, sorted, and packed for a new home.

Sounds daunting to some; to others, it is a great relief to have a target date to make changes. Michelle Wright of Wide Open Spaces has crafted a niche business of "heirloom rescuing" and "money wrangling," helping farm folks in northeastern Alberta make the transition to a new lifestyle.

Here are Wright's tips:

5 Tips for Planning Your Move Off the Farm

1. Get Started by Focusing on the Farm Piece

In our case, the farm is staying in the family, just with new faces in the yard. For farm folks who are vacating and selling, they have more layers of issues, including finances, organization, and making transitional plans. Wright has a background in stakeholder relations in the oil patch, so she uses those skills to help folks focus on one piece of the move at a time.

2. List Out the Many Things That You Want to Accomplish

Wright works at the kitchen table and builds relationships with the landowners. She can remove firearms since she has her firearms safety certificate. She is on a first name basis with the landfill folks and has trained to remove hazardous materials and dangerous goods. She knows the correct disposal for lots of stuff and has metal guys who clear up bush loads of steel and iron and take it away. Their fee is usually the value of the load on the trailer.

3. Know Your Social Service Network

Many adult children live far away from the home farm that is up for sale, and they don't want to be driving or flying "home" every weekend of their precious summer to be dealing with all of mom and dad's possessions (a.k.a. junk)! Wright lines up social service connections and food banks locally who can benefit from the household effects. She gets called in when the dad starts giving away boxes of stuff while he promises to get things cleaned up, but somehow dad never gets the de-cluttering job finished.

4. Have Realistic Expectations

Farmers rarely move. Over the course of 40 to 60 years, they can accumulate a pile of stuff. You've probably watched the picker shows on TV where guys hunt for treasure, but you don't have time for this. Wright feels you need 18 months to downsize. She coaches her families gently over and over again saying, "Let go." Letting go is a coaching strategy. You need to be able to let go of things so that you can create new space for a new chapter in your life. Wright is careful to ask, "Where are your treasures?" and learns the story about the objects. When the clients say, "I am not ready to let go," then Wright asks, "What are you ready for?"

5. Get Another Perspective on Your Stuff

Wright has downsized a grain bin full of used washing machines. The objection from the hoarder was "if something breaks I might need a part!" Imagine all the generations of stuff in layers in the farmhouse. Get rid of what you don't need, then give treasures to grandkids and share the story of that treasure while you are alive.

Tips for Decluttering Your Home

As a home economist who enjoys practical re-purposing of found objects, I am drawn to de-cluttering articles and books. The hot one on the market these days, which I have read, is *The Life-Changing Magic of Tidying Up: The Japanese Art of Decluttering and Organizing* by Marie Kondo. Here are some of her tips.

- **Start with Clothing:** Kondo starts with clothes first, by discarding all at once, intensely and completely. I know that when my aunt died, my uncle could not move a thing, even five years later when it was his turn to move to a new home. Do your family a favor by making large donations to the local thrift store. Start with clothing and the rest will follow.

- **Remember Your Motivation:** Have a picture on the fridge of your new home or ideal new location. A vision of what you are moving toward can inspire you to keep throwing away or giving away the pieces of your old life chapter that you don't need to carry along.

- **Share with Others:** You can also help your items find new homes. My mother-in-law set up an 8-foot table that was the FREE zone, and each time she had visitors, they had to scan the table for treasures to take home with them. Her large book collection was a great gift to life-long learners who appreciated her generosity.

- **Take Pictures Instead:** I have deep emotional connections to stuff; my age five black and white oxford shoes are in my freezer room on a rafter. UGH. They don't bring me joy, but a photo of them would likely be more realistic to keep.

- **Keep Only What Brings You Joy:** Kondo suggests that "during the selection process, if you come across something that does not spark joy but that you just can't bring yourself to throw away, stop for a moment and ask yourself, "Am I having trouble getting rid of this because of an attachment to the past or because of a fear for the future?" Our ownership patterns reflect what we value.

Borrow Kondo's book from your library and be inspired to start downsizing. Leaving a tidy estate is a great gift to your heirs. Taking the things with you that bring joy will bless your new home in town and give you a fresh start for the next chapter beyond the farm.

Notes:

_____

_____

_____

_____

_____

_____

_____

_____

_____

Chapter 20:

Leaving the Farm: Signs That It Is Time to Go and What to Do Next

It's summer, and you are wondering if this is the last season for you working on the farm because you are tired of chronic fighting.

No matter how hard you have worked at trying to get along and make things work, sometimes the conflict situation cannot be resolved. You need to move on, realizing that you can only control your own actions. To continue in the muck takes endless energy, and it is draining you.

You can't fix other people. You may try to influence them, but they are stonewalling, broken, or facing mental health issues that are barriers to functioning well.

You need to let go.

Signs That It Is Time to Go

Only you can decide if it is time to leave the farm, and you should take time to reflect before you make a final decision. The following may be signs that it is, in fact, time to go. How many of these apply to you?

- Trouble sleeping over a long period of time, more than a year, because you have gone through all the seasons of the farm, and nothing has changed. A year is enough time to think things over and make a shift.

- You cannot stop crying, kicking or have uncontrollable anger or prolonged sadness. Your stomach pains and headaches are signs that your body is not dealing well with internalized stress.

- Your relationship with your spouse or partner and your children is rocky because of the farm team stress.

- You cannot stop talking about the fights, and the conversations keep reverting to the same old story.

- People who care about you are telling you that they are sick of hearing about it, and they are concerned you are staying in the mess.

- It costs you financially. Farming should be profitable, and not a sinkhole for your outside resources.

- There is chronic conflict on the farm team. It may be time to ask yourself "Why am I still here?"

- You have tried farm coaching, mediation or counseling, using outside interventions, and things still don't change.

- The grass is starting to look greener outside the farm fence, so you are starting to see other options for your life.

- You have deep value conflict issues, knowing you cannot negotiate value differences. For example, younger families typically put a high value on work-life balance, while the founders often are workaholics, so the work ethic value will never be negotiated well. You need to accept that core values drive the way people do things and frame their expectations.

- Your vision for the growth or sustainability of the farm is highly different from your business partners. This indicates it may be time to farm separately or follow other pursuits.

- A farm team member is violent, abusive, manipulative, or has a huge sense of entitlement. Sometimes this is an indicator that you need to leave quickly and end that farming relationship.

What to Do Next? 10 Questions to Ask Yourself

If you decide that it is in fact time to leave the farm, first step back and think things through logically. Some questions to ask are:

What is important to you now and what do you hope will happen?

Identify where you want to be, and set your current priorities. Set specific goals for each aspect of your life, like economic goals, family goals, and time goals.

What will family relationships look like when you leave the farm?

Know that you don't have to stay so physically close or emotionally close to them. You get to decide the healthy boundaries of the relationship. You may need some "cooling off" time. If relationships are super nasty, you may not be able to continue any communication or only have very limited contact with certain criteria.

What are your options for exiting?

This is tough and complex depending on how intertwined you are with the farm business. My experience is that few farm families have operating or partnership agreements that clearly spell out how one partner leaves the business.

Sort out the financial implications of leaving. What will be the assets you take with you? What is your new income stream going to be? Have your updated your resume or sought assistance from an employment counselor?

Where will you live next?

Many farms own all the houses on the property. Leaving the family business can also mean leaving your house behind. Just the threat of looking for a new home in town, or the next community, may be the tipping point to start a reconciling conversation to force change.

How can you continue your family relationships when all is said and done?

Richness in a relationship comes with hard work and intentionality. Grandparents long to see their grand-kids and farming sons and daughters who leave want some connection on their own terms. What baby steps can you take to build up your emotional bank account with your family? Is your spouse willing to engage in this process with you?

What are your timelines and deadlines for each element of the change?

For example, in the next two weeks, "I am writing my resume, and looking online or asking around for jobs."

Look at new training possibilities and allow yourself to dream. There are new opportunities ahead.

Make an appointment with the accountant to figure out the asset mix and financial implications of leaving the farm partnership.

Consider using a counselor or mediator to define the healthy boundaries you are willing to accept with your family relationships.

Who can help you adjust to the changes?

The change may be difficult. Do you have friends you can network with or a support group to help you through the transition? This might be tricky if all your friends are very intertwined with your business life. Perhaps professionals, or far away friends will give a clearer perspective.

What do you need to do to let go?

Having mental closure will help you with the transition, so it's time to grieve the losses and celebrate your successes. Any time you move into a new phase of your life, you need to let go of things in order to create space for new opportunities. You may have sadness, anger, and sense of loss as you grieve what could have been. You should also be proud of the accomplishments that you have achieved in your time on the farm, however small they may be.

How can I ensure that I will stick to my decision?

If your decision is well thought out and agreed upon with your spouse, then you should follow through. Tough decisions have tough consequences, and this is not going to be easy. Resist the urge to cave in.

How Others Might React to You Leaving the Farm

If you have decided to leave the farm, one concern you may have is how others will react to your decision. Understanding the particular reactions you may face will help prepare you.

1. Foot stomping and door crashing.

Anger will erupt since you have messed up the "status quo." Anger comes fear, hurt, and frustration with the loss of relationship and power.

2. Exclusion.

Exclusion from the will, family gatherings, and "inside family information" may occur when people grasp for ways to inflict hurt or revenge.

Threats and bad behavior are symptoms of a larger problem of not being able to adapt to change and let go graciously.

3. Sometimes people need time to process change and figure it out.

Behavior may improve a few months down the road when the family reaches a new kind of equilibrium.

4. Relief and gratefulness may be expressed when all is said and done.

Imagine what the neighbors might say, but pay attention to what immediate family is expressing. A middle-aged farm woman once thanked me as the coach, for "giving her her husband back" once the farm separation was complete.

5. The neighbors are going to talk.

Know what the family script is for the exit; in other words, "What are we going to tell our friends and neighbors?" The more united and positive everyone on the farm team can be, the better the transition. The script is what you have decided to say in one sentence when people ask about what is going on with the farm. Here is a sample script: "We are making changes that benefit all of our family, and we are looking forward to the new chapter for our farm."

6. Non-farm heirs and siblings will also have an opinion.

What is your plan for how much detail and information they need to have?

Leaving the farm is a tough decision to make, but if it is truly time to go, then you should not hold yourself back from the opportunities that lie ahead. Do you have a story about how you successfully exited? I'd love to hear your stories about exiting well.

Notes:

_____

_____

_____

_____

_____

_____

_____

_____

_____

Chapter 21:

Farm Widow Business Savvy: Preparing for the Unfortunate

Another fatal farm accident reports hit my ears, just after presenting to a large group. "Another young farm widow joins a club she does not ever want to belong to; I wonder how she will manage the farm, her family, herself," I wonder.

Now that I belong to the "Freedom 59" club, I am not retiring from my coaching practice or my supportive role to my farming husband. I do, however, think about how I would manage 5000 acres and a seed business if Wes were to die soon. How would I even prepare to be a young widow? (59 is young, 86 is the new life expectancy for women in Canada).

It is not something any of us likes to think about but is a possibility that we should all prepare for. It is a process that requires much courage and here are some ways to help you walk through the preparation and planning process.

10 Steps to Help Prepare for the Unfortunate Chance of Becoming a Farm Widow

1. Talk about what you would do.

Share "what if" scenarios with your spouse so that you have a clear indication of their intent and wishes for you to carry on. Consider whom you would hire as part of your team of advisors. Find good recommendations via word of mouth referrals and the business directory of Canadian Association of Farm Advisors. Use this year to plan a calendar of events of farm activities and deadlines that keep you up to date with farm management. Visit the accountant with your spouse for tax planning.

2. Develop a relationship with a financial planner whom you as a couple both trust and respect.

This is looking at your lifestyle income needs, your personal investment risk tolerance, and your goals for ensuring your debt, estate tax liabilities, and long-term care or critical illness possibilities. I expect that you know how to write cheques and balance the accounts. Unfortunately, I have met women my age who never touched the family's finances! UGH! Get a clear picture of what you actually spend on living, because, as a widow, you'll be negotiating cash flow with your successors who also have living needs.

3. Update and review your insurance.

I am hearing stories about men who are outliving their insurance policies, and not renewing them due to high premiums. They do not have the $600K cash from the proceeds they intended to share with non-business heirs. They do not want the farm to pay the premiums. In another case, the dad canceled the insurance without letting the family know, and you can bet the grieving family was more than shocked when that uninsured fellow dropped dead due to a heart attack a few years later.

4. Ask your accountant all the dumb questions you need to.

There are no dumb questions, just lots of assumptions that are waiting for clarification. My chartered accountant is concerned when she interviews farm widows who have never engaged even at a basic level of caring about the farm finances. It is time to learn more about the balance sheets, debt service and asset values you are going to have to make decisions on! I am saddened to hear from wealthy widows who had no clue how rich they were and now are not able to embrace a financial strategy to enjoy their status as their health is failing. Do you have a poverty mentality based on false assumptions about your net worth? Do you have titles with your name on them?

5. Check to see that you have an enduring power of attorney with an adult child you trust, and an alternate.

If you are a widow and become incapacitated from making decisions, then who do you trust to take care of you? Do this before you are assessed with mental health issues and are still thinking clearly.

6. Make a life binder manual to have all your documents in order.

This would include any contact information for advisors, plumbers, electricians, etc. You can download forms to fill in at www.rightrisk.org. I've written about this before, and my binder is started but needs a blizzard day to get done. As the executor of an estate, it helps to know where all the important papers are. Also, don't forget to write down necessary computer passwords.

Go to my website to request the "Because I love You tool" at www.elainefroese.com/contact.

7. Encourage your husband to write down all the things in his head that the farm needs to know for ongoing farm management.

Men hate to do this. How can you make it easier? I have purchased Dick Wittman's consulting binder which is full of templates and operating procedures. This might be a great task to tackle with your young successors, who would like to see things on paper while Dad is still alive and well to put his wisdom into text. The young widow that I mentioned has a lot of cows to feed, and the ration ratios died with the farmer. What information needs to be shared with your farm team to pass along the managerial tasks smoothly?

8. Book a spa day when you can celebrate getting all your affairs in order.

Alternatively, buy your favorite book. Have something to look forward to, maybe a date with your hubby to tell him how thankful you are for his love and provision. Men (and women) have a tough go on farms and carry a lot of stress around being successful providers. They need some appreciation now, not just at their eulogy.

9. Start planning your funeral, and ask the funeral director for a template of the invoice your family is going to receive.

You'd be shocked at all the "add-ons" of services, and making pre-arrangements can be helpful so that decisions do not need to be made in the emotionally charged days of fresh grief. Ask your husband to tell stories about his prized possessions, and then list the names and articles that he wishes to gift. Better yet, give the gifts with a warm hand.

10. Ask the next generation to help you build a digital DVD collection of farm photos and family shots that diarize the legacy your farm family has enjoyed over the years.

The story is not finished yet, but start working on the chapters of your life story now. When my dad died, I relied heavily on a creative memories photo album that I had created for his 75th birthday. Get working on those photo archives and relive the great memories of cherishing your family.

Notes:

_____

_____

_____

_____

_____

_____

_____

Chapter 22:

What Will Happen to Your Personal Property?

In July of 2011, we took my failing father for one last tour of his shop, farm, and fields for his 85th birthday. Unknown to us, he would not be here for Christmas 2012, and we, as a family, are going through our years of "firsts" without Dad. Mom has been gone for 14 years.

As I sort through cherished possessions for the grandkids and siblings, it strikes me that there are many things I am thankful that I did while my folks were still around. On the other hand, I am not thrilled with some of the ways the non-titled possessions were dealt with. I wish I could ask my parents to tell me about the gold cuff links with my granddad's initials. I never knew they existed until the cleaning day came.

The Stories Behind Your Possessions

When my mom passed, I started giving away her jewelry to my cousins. They chose pieces that they liked and said it was an unexpected treat to get to pick something from my Mom's box that reminded them of her kindness to them as new brides.

For me, the things that are hardest to let go of are the mementos that hold the story of a special trip. I have a Paua shell in my bathroom that Dad brought home from New Zealand in the fifties. It has more meaning to me now since I just visited New Zealand in December after Dad died. I was also looking for a special Maori box of his, but it has been lost.

These examples demonstrate that it is not the possessions themselves but rather the stories behind them that truly make your possessions special.

When passing on your property, don't forget the importance of passing on the stories too.

Who Gets Personal Property When You are Gone?

"Who gets personal property is an issue frequently ignored until a crisis occurs. Decision making becomes challenging when people are grieving, selling the home they grew up in, and facing the increased dependence of an elder," says University of Minnesota professor Marlene Stum.

Your farm shed, shop or garage might be storing some of those personal items that don't come with a title or deed (thus they are called non-titled items) to indicate who officially owns them. I've heard folks talk about buying the home place "lock stock and barrel" only to discover that siblings have been sneaking away wagon wheels, lanterns, and other antiques. Toys, tools, jewelry, musical instruments, linens, needlework, furniture, dishes, pets, collectibles, books, and sporting equipment are all examples of non-titled property that can be disputed.

So, what do you do?

Spell Out Your Personal Property Wishes Now

Professor Stum recommends making a list of your personal property wishes while you are still alive. Here are her tips.

- **Share the story that goes with the item, and relay the family history.** I just gave away a rusty lantern with a glass in great condition. This made a garage sale hound very happy, and I let go of it because I did not know its history.

- **Personal belongings hold sensitive feelings and memories.** It is curious to me that both my son and nephew were keen to have grandma's candy dish. Don't assume you know the memories attached to certain items. Ask!

- **Fair is defined differently by different folks.** In the TV show *Storage Wars,* the buyer gets the contents of the storage container and hopes to find treasure. When farm families start taking things out of a family home while the owner is in a personal care home, or antiques start disappearing from the farm shed, there is lots of fuel for conflict. Oldest son gets this, or oldest daughter gets that is not really a workable formula in modern times. To prevent family fights, it is best to talk about what you want to do with your possessions and make a list of who gets what and when.

- **Ask each person in your family what is special to them, and ask them to explain why.** The best practice is to have a family meeting and discuss what each heir is interested in and why. We did this with my father before he became ill. It was helpful to the executor to know what the other siblings were thinking and wanting.

- **Make a list.** With laptops, it is easy to take notes and have an emailed list to all parties for future reference. You might also want to take this one step further with the adult grandchildren. Your list of preferred destinations of possessions upon your departure from earth can be filed with your executor.

- **Consider sharing some of your cherished possessions while you are still alive.** I am still of the opinion that gifts that are given to you by a warm hand with the story of the gift communicated too are way more meaningful than gifts given by the cold hand of the estate. Be a trendsetter in your community and start down-sizing your collectibles and shed stuff while you are mentally and physically able to make a difference in how you dispose of your possessions. Put unwanted items in a consignment auction sale. Use the proceeds to celebrate a special time with your family.

- **When there is conflict, use straws or draw names in order to take turns picking who gets what.** One family used monopoly money to bid on items that were in dispute. I also know families who wanted very little in terms of "things" because they were rich in a relationship with their parents. In that case, the local thrift stores got a lot of treasures to sell.

- **Take digital photos of special items, and then give them away for someone else to dust.** You will still have the memory, and no one can take that from you.

Start Decluttering Today

Disposing of the contents of the farm is a long process, so start this summer.

- Call the steel guy and find out what a trailer load of dead augers and cultivator shovels might be worth. Our three trailers fetched $500 each a while back.

- Think about being charitable. One family's RV went to a camp, and they received a charitable receipt.

- Feed the burn pile with junk that is no one's treasure. Ask permission to give away things after you've consulted with all possible owners. I am still not popular for once giving away a special fishing rod without permission!

- Have a spot for hazardous waste and things that need to go the refuse/landfill site, i.e. the dump! Our dump has a "free store" area where folks can scavenge for treasure. Make sure you come home from the dump with an empty pickup.

Someone once said that clutter is energy constipation. I suppose there are a few farm sheds across the prairies that are bulging with stuff. Think of the new energy you'll have when you walk into the old barn, shop or garage to see things tidied up, and all the treasures passed on to those who will actually appreciate their value.

Notes:

_____

_____

_____

_____

_____

_____

_____

_____

_____

SUCCESSION

(Business Continuance or Transition)

Chapter 23:

8 Internal Conflicts that Stall Succession Plans

"I wasn't able to talk for over two years about what happened with my grandfather," a young farmer confides as he describes a bitter battle over the transition of land titles from his father's father to him.

I am concerned about the many threads of conversations across farm audiences that weave a sad tale of loss, grief, and exasperation with those farmers who are over eighty and are not finishing their farming careers well.

Leaving a lasting legacy as a farmer is not just about money and land. It also involves how you wish to be remembered for your character, and how you want to resolve conflicts before your passing. Do you want a family tree that is broken or one that is flourishing? Do you realize that the next generation and the younger farmers are just as passionate about being a great farmer as you were in your late twenties?

What is stopping you from gifting and transferring with a warm, open, and generous hand on top, rather than a clenched fist?

I have my hunches.

8 Internal Conflicts that Stall Succession Plans

You think that money equals security.

You are afraid that you will not have enough to live on for the next 20 years, even though you have $500K in the bank, and shares in the company. You aren't even enjoying the wealth you have now because your health keeps you housebound.

Ralph Waldo Emerson was onto something when he said, "Your health is your wealth."

Your pension income, your debt-free living, and your personal wealth will keep you going. Why not transfer those farm assets and see the pride of ownership shine on your grandson's face? Great family relationships ensure that even if you are close to dying broke, your loved ones will not "put you out on the street...or gravel road!"

You are afraid of losing control.

Your friends are all dying, and you certainly cannot control that. Facing death is hard for you, so you deny the invitations to update wills and invoke the Power of Attorney that will protect your affairs with your trusted advisor now. Is holding on the only thing that gives you a sense of power and control over your own destiny? Yikes. I would choose to be rich in a relationship over being a lonely land baron any day. Families are supposed to be a sanctuary of love and nurture, not nasty fight centers of conflict avoidance and deep hurt.

How about extending the hand of forgiveness and forging a newly reconciled chapter in your family? How about dying without any regrets? These are things that you do have control over.

You fear that hard times could happen again.

You recall the depression as a young person who struggled. You are proud of the wealth you have built. You might sense that others see you as greedy, but you don't care anymore. Your heart is so hardened that not even your wife's pleading for family connection and harmony can get you to budge. Your word rules the day. You think interest and debt are evil, but do you realize that the transfer of assets to your son, daughter, and grandchildren could be a big boost to the debt servicing capacity of the next generation? Your young grandchild can get young farmer rebates and loans that he or she can manage. They weren't born in the early eighties to remember high-interest rates, but they are financially astute and smart managers. Please trust them!

You have trouble communicating.

You are desperate to have some form of communication, but unfortunately, the chaotic conversations of TV sitcoms replace the voices of your family members.

We honor the fact that you have worked hard, struggled, and overcome many of the stresses of agriculture. We don't see workaholic and family dictatorship as a badge of honor. The younger generation is much more collaborative in their approach. If do not wish to help them get started in building equity with the transfer of your asset, they will seek non-family joint venture partners.

You worry about your legacy.

What do you want to be written on your headstone? How would you like to be remembered? Are there special possessions like a gun collection, tools, or cars that you might like to share stories about with your beneficiaries? There is a song that says, "when it is all said and done, things will just not matter."

Pinball Clemons spoke to the Canadian Young Farmers Forum 2012 AGM, and he said farmers are superheroes. He also noted that strong, healthy families are the foundation of everything else going right in the world. Our rural towns need strong families and farm businesses in order to be sustainable and thrive. Imagine if every farmer in their eighties took their legacy to heart, and did the things to finish well.

You think it is all or nothing.

Wealth can be transferred in stages, but a plan needs to be legally binding and well thought out for tax planning and meeting expectations of all generations. It is not a "you win; I lose" type of scenario. There are many creative options available when you use a great team of advisors who understand your intent and why you are making or avoiding certain decisions. Farmers are fiercely independent entrepreneurs. The new crop of leaders is going to use a collaborative approach, team up with non-family and seek out innovation.

You are afraid of change.

Remember how good it felt to finally get that new or "gently used" piece of equipment to make your farm tasks easier and be more efficient in your work? The folks who seek new tools early are called the early adaptors, and they are the ones that see profits first, long before the laggards, the last ones to change or even know what happened. Embrace change. Be someone who is ahead of the game, rather than the unwise one who is left behind. Use common sense and the wisdom of your years to be adaptable.

You worry that there will no longer be a place for you on the farm.

Your role as you age is now different, but there will always be a place for you on the farm. Take on the position of an elder mentor. Be the fellow who folks like to come to for a historical perspective on how to be resilient, and yet practically optimistic about the future of agriculture.

I have some very wise, well-balanced over-70 farm coach clients. I just wish I could clone their skills and personalities to inject a sense of hope for those younger farmers who are feeling so stuck with a grandparent that refuses to finish well.

These internal conflicts can be overcome. What is your choice going to be? Choose to resolve the conflict and leave a great farm family legacy.

Notes:

_____

_____

_____

_____

Chapter 24:

Defining and Discussing "The Plan"

As the farming population of boomers ages so does the over eighty crowd. These aging patriarchs and matriarchs are still ruling farms, some with a heavy hand. This is not a happy situation for the grandchildren in their 20s who are dreaming of establishing their farming careers after college. It is also the cause of many sleepless nights and marital strife for the couple that is caught in the middle between a stubborn farming father and growing adult children who want to know what "THE PLAN" is.

Let's Define "The Plan"

"The Plan" is knowing when granddad is going to transfer ownership of assets to the younger generation. The lawyers may have cautioned him about not "ruling from the grave," but he is keen on tying up his assets for as long as possible and not transferring title to land or moving shares. Is this due to fear of loss of wealth, avoidance of conflict, or just the stubborn price to keep a tight fist of control till death?

"The Plan" impacts all members of the farm family differently.

Grandparents Over 80

Gracious grandparents have ample personal wealth to live out their days on this earth with style and dignity. They are happy to shift ownership of the business with a warm hand, not a cold one. These folks grew up in times of depression and great financial strife, but they are not going to let their "money scripts" tie up the growth and passions of their grandchildren. They also will not be bullied into helping keep all of their own children economically equal because they know that is a foolish approach to fairness.

The plan also involves finances for assisted living or long-term care, should the over 80 parents need that kind of care. Wills are updated, enduring powers of attorney in place, and a healthcare directive is signed and ready to go.

Parents in Their 50s and 60s

The next piece of the plan is for the "sandwiched" couple in their late 50s and early 60s. For 25 to 30 years now they have scrimped and deferred gratification in order to grow equity outside the grasp of grandpa. They have also created and expanded grandad's wealth by farming his assets, providing him with a handsome income. The only trouble is, they are tired, want a new chapter of life, and are in a quandary as to how to help set up the next generation when they are still stuck with debt and not enough assets they can call their own.

The 50s/60s couple needs a personal financial snapshot. If they are going to stay in their current housing, they just saved $400K that is not needed for a new home in town. If they continue to travel for short periods and live simply enjoying grandchildren, things look pretty sweet. The part of the certainty of the plan that escapes them is the date that they will inherit the grandparent's assets, and how much of those assets will be going to non-farm siblings. Ouch. Wouldn't it be nice if the assets were all transferred before death so that each person could get on with their business growth? Or at least have a greater share of farm's net income going to the folks who are slaving away in the fields and the barn?

Grandchildren in Their 20s and 30s

Then the plan extends to the grandchildren who are the fresh new labor and energy of the farm. They are future business heirs and partners. They will work much harder when they actually own something and have what is called "skin in the game." Debt servicing has a way of making the youngest generation pay attention to costs, market returns, and cash flow. They learn to crunch numbers and work smarter, not just harder. They are also marrying at this stage and having babies, which calls for family time. All work and no play is the perfect set-up for early divorce and grumpy people.

It's Time to Discuss "The Plan"

Stop the procrastination on your farm now. Have a joint meeting with your key advisors and the eighty-year-olds on your farm. You can no longer be a slave to a system that is not fair. Accountants can plan for tax efficiency. Lawyers can draw up new share agreements, wills, and powers of attorney. Financial planners can give the 80-year-olds financial certainty and security with their pensions and personal wealth kept for their needs. Coaches can facilitate the courageous conversations where each generation talks about needs, wants, and the timeline to get things done. Counselors can deal with grief, loss and divorce healing.

Aging parents may suffer from unwise decision making when their minds start to fail, and dementia becomes a reality. Boomers die from heart and stroke disease, cancer, and accidents, which can leave the remaining spouse in a difficult situation if there is no contingency plan to follow except fighting with the in-laws for control of business assets.

The young farmers can't stand the "pain of not knowing the plan" and being in limbo. They are wired to have action and to have results.

Wise farm families are always talking, listening, and making adjustment as necessary to the business plan, succession timeline, and the estate concerns. This is not a one-time event, but a journey.

Unfortunately, I have encountered far too many over 80 men and women who are wielding undeserved control over the future of the farm. Please embrace change as a good process, and ask for help in making the changes need to preserve a happy farm family legacy, not a war of words and battle for power and control.

Act your age. It is time to shift your mindset from the control of the business to creating a harmonious legacy.

Life is short. Death is certain. Make a new plan now!

Notes:

_____

_____

_____

_____

_____

_____

_____

_____

_____

Chapter 25:

The 3 C's for Farm Ownership Transfer

Founders typically want to know where their income streams will be after they let go of power and control of management and/or ownership. They also have marital conflict about home residence issues, and how to be fair to non-business heirs.

The next generation can't wait to gain equity, quota, and more decision-making power. Young farmers are smart, tech-savvy, and want to have their opinions heard and respected by parents. They also need certainty that the timelines for transfer and succession agreements will be honored. Add the conflict dynamics of a new spouse, and you have many interesting conversations ahead!

Last November at the World Holstein Symposium in Toronto, I spoke about the three key things needed for great farm ownership transfers; clarity, certainty, and commitment to act.

3 C's for Farm Ownership Transfer

Clarity

I encourage you to converse in a sit-down business meeting with all the generations on your farm. Be clear with each about the vision for growth, as well as the roles and expectations for each worker. You might like to start out with "I am just curious what your vision of our farm looks like." If the tension is too tight, hire a coach or facilitator to walk you through conflict resolution. We all perform better when we are clear about what is expected of us.

Certainty

People are jazzed, and business is profitable when everyone on the team gets things done in a timely fashion, and folks are certain of the deadlines or timelines for action. Most next generation farmers are extremely frustrated because they are stuck in what William Bridges calls the "neutral zone." Put your farm transition plan in drive and get unstuck. The best way to do this is to talk about the conflicting needs and wants that have to be reconciled. Build your team of advisors to help you map out where the farm is going, and when. What is the date that you plan to give equity shares to your son or daughter who farms with you? When will the next generation be the main manager?

Commitment to Act

I am wearing a red bracelet that says, "my commitment" as a reminder to act on business goals. What are you using as a catalyst for those courageous conversations that you need to have in order to put new management and ownership agreements in place? Are you stalling because of fear about fairness to the non-business heirs?

Non-business heirs refer to the status of your adult children who are not on your farm team as workers and future owners. Book an appointment with your financial planner and accountant to find ways to create cash flow for building your personal wealth bubble. You need options to take care of your income streams first, your lifestyle plan as you age, and then your estate plan. Face your fears about fairness, and get plans in place!

A Chinese proverb says, "Talk does not cook rice." Talking is a great place to start. Be a good listener with a learner mindset, not a judgment mindset. Make this a great year by talking, committing and then acting to "Do the Tough Things Right" on your farm.

Notes:

_____

_____

_____

_____

_____

_____

_____

_____

_____

_____

Chapter 26:

Understanding the Next Generation of Farmers

During the 2015 AgExcellence Conference, young farmers contributed to a Twitter feed called "We Wish Parents Understood." Although I was not able to attend, I did see the feed, and now I'd like to express my take on their comments based on years of coaching young farmers.

The List of "We Wish Parents Understood"

1. Work-life balance.

2. This is 2015.

3. Let's get a plan.

4. Parents are entitled to retire.

5. Partners get to choose; they don't have to be involved.

My Reflections

Work-Life Balance

I recall one wife accosting me at a farm show to say thank-you for the best February birthday she had ever had. Apparently, her husband was in my audience and heard my encouragement to "date your wife" – show up with cards, flowers, and an invitation for a restaurant meal. He followed through for the first time in their 24-year marriage, and she was shocked but thrilled to be cherished in that way.

I often tell audiences that the next generation is not willing to put in the long work hours that the parents have, and the heads nod in agreement.

The next generation is looking for work-life balance but, unfortunately, I think "balance" is a misnomer, as it is something that is never done and always needs to be negotiated in the family. It is also tied to the question of farm growth. Is this farm big enough? Can we sustain the pace of work already required? Could we become more efficient with what we already have? How can we get a workaholic father/founder to realize that "we are not him" ever?

As with most tough issues, this one requires communication about reasonable expectations. The urgency here is to protect the marriage and family values of each couple. If the farming son values tucking his son into bed with stories, grandpa better stop fuming in the field. If the marriage crumbles due to lack of attention, you have a bigger threat to handle, and it is called "divorce." All generations should be intentional about building fun into the farm week.

That Was Then; This Is Now

I suspect this relates to my phrase "that was then, and this is now." Things are different. Different is not wrong it is just different. What is it about the new ways of doing things in 2015 that threatens the founders? What exactly does the next generation mean by "this is 2015?"

Over the years, things have changed though. Some things, like neighborly visits and parties, aren't happening anymore in my neighborhood. "This is 2015" also speaks to new ways and approaches to farming. I see this with the next generation being quicker to outsource tasks like bookkeeping or custom work that better matches the skill set they want to offer to the farm. It also means embracing new technologies and using the computer to analyze data for better decision making. Take away my son's internet for research, and he would be crippled.

Let's Get a Plan

Young farmers have high anxiety and stress with not knowing what "The Plan" is for their future, including options to build equity and create financial security for their growing families. "The Plan" can seem complex, but we can make it simpler.

Break your plans down to specific areas: a lifestyle plan that outlines the income stream needed for family living for both generations; a succession plan with timelines as to when the management and ownership pieces will start shifting; a business plan for the vision of the farm in the next 5 years; and an estate plan to get wills updated and power of attorney set.

There...was that complicated? No, just a series of plans that are inter-related. Contact me regarding my $10 binder tabs, and I'll get you started.

Parents Are Entitled to Retire

Parents are entitled to retire, but 30 percent of farmers in Iowa never do! I prefer the term reinvention, as the parents' roles change to suit the needs of the new management of the younger generation. Compassionate farm dads and moms make great mentors, and the young farmers appreciate gracious. Wise elders are happy to make collaborative decisions with the energy of youth and the wisdom of experience.

If parents have created a "personal wealth bubble" outside of the farm's accounts, they may have funds to play, travel, and gift to non-business heirs without creating too much stress on the farm's cash flow. The main point here is to have a full-blown exploration with the parents as to what a good day to them is like for them on the farm in their re-invention years. The message from my 70-something audience in Alberta was "don't wait until after 65 to travel, do it earlier while you still have your health to enjoy it!" I enjoy the millennials who tell me that their parents deserve to enjoy the fruits of their labor of over 40 years, and they desire that the parents have fun!

Partners Get to Choose; They Don't Have to Be Involved

In 2016 a good percentage of young farmers have two jobs, one on the farm and one away. Some folks who are married to farmers choose not to get involved in the farm business at all. They create a very clear boundary that states, "I married you, not the farm!" Older folks don't like to hear this. In their perfect world, everyone on the farm, regardless of gender or roles, pitches in, especially in the busy seasons of spring planting and harvest.

My coaching conversations have revealed amazing incomes and energy for other careers that young women especially are not appreciated for. Their off-farm income allows the farm spouse to churn funds back into farm growth, yet their contribution of cash flow for family living is not appreciated or recognized by the founders.

Again, the best remedy for this misalignment of values is to have courageous, transparent conversations about what roles work for you and which ones you cannot embrace.

These insights from AgEXCONF 2015 give us a lot to think about as we embrace young farmers. Understanding the things that they "wish" we'd know will make the transition easier for these future leaders of the farm.

Notes:

_____

_____

_____

_____

_____

_____

_____

_____

Chapter 27:

Achieving Mutually Beneficial Landlord Relationships

I am extremely grateful for the three neighbors who showed up with three extra combines to harvest on the last sunny Saturday of September; it really made a huge difference in reducing the stress on our farm. When I relayed this story to an easterner, he said, "Wow, they still do that out there! Neighbors here are so competitive for land; that never happens anymore!"

So, are you cultivating harmonious relationships with the landowner's next door, or are you just hoping they will read your mind and know what your farm vision is for expanding your land base with your successor?

How Are You Doing with Landowner Relationships?

Some pro-active farmers are doing a "retiring producer needs assessment" with older farmers and planting the seeds of an ongoing conversation. They ask questions about the $ /year income stream that is needed, if there is a plan in place, and whether or not the farmer has an "exit plan." Retiring farmers are typically really concerned that they know they should have a plan to exit, but in reality, there is no plan. Sometimes this conversation can last five years. This is not a "hostile takeover" kind of talk, but one lead by the aging farmer, with grace and respect.

Are you working at introducing your successor to the landowners that you deal with? Farmers like to know who is going to be caring for their land, and they want great stewards to farm their land well. The retiring farmer also wants to do business with someone who is transparent, honest, trustworthy and pays their bills on time. The renter also wants to make sure that the landowners feel like they are "well taken care of."

Do you know who your "best prospects" are to rent or buy land from? Some keener negotiators are talking to their best prospects at least monthly. They are "talking to them every chance they get and also trying to create chances to talk with them!" This is relationship selling, mostly done on the phone, sometimes by text. The aging farmers at community meetings for the school, curling club, fair, 4-H, farm groups, and church are also not left unnoticed.

Cautions

When trying to forge relationships with other landowners, there are several things you should keep in mind.

- Be sensitive to what the aging landowner is going through. Some folks do not want their land to change hands until they die.

- Pick the right "tailgate time" to have a casual conversation about the farmer's plans for the land. This is not community news; this is a confidential talk.

- Custom working the land gives you an opportunity to show how well you farm and care for the earth.

- See if there are economic enticements such as helping the aging farmer sell some of his equipment or get it ready for auction.

- Consider finder's fees for those folks who understand the relationship selling process who can give you workable referrals.

- Beware of people "pretending" to be deal makers when they really don't want to have conversations about renting or selling. Be sure that the farmer has the ability to make a rental or sale decision.

An 8-Step Process

To build up your relationships with other landowners, it is wise to follow a plan. I have offered a process you can use below.

1. Start with a list of prospects with whom you would like to form relationships. Good solid relationships with retiring farmers may take years to build.

2. Help solve the retiring farmer's problems by selling outdated equipment or doing custom work for them. Preface your comments with "when you feel ready to retire…"

3. Have your agreements in writing. (I recall a farm family with many elderly landowners who didn't like paper contracts, but the new generation of young farmers made written agreements a condition of renting, clearly just their business policy.)

4. Make sure you have all the substantial conversations with all the important decision makers present at the same time.

5. Set the expectations ahead of time for the assessment survey, "I'd like to ask you a set of questions that may sound "hokey", but they are important for all of us to be clear about what everyone needs out of this land rent process." The assessment survey is created by the buyer/renter to get a clear understanding of what the retiring farmer needs.

6. Look inside yourself. Are you a good manager? Do you have great management capability and empathy with a heart to care about your neighbor's well-being?

7. Sometimes an outside advisor like an accountant or agronomist may have the facilitation skills to bring the interested parties together for a "social" discussion of the possibilities. This works if the parties have similar values and can say "I like the way you think; you think like I think."

8. When the terms of the agreement are put together, seek out separate legal counsel and get the deal done.

Many retiring farmers are happy when they know they have put their land into the care of good hands. Some exiting dads take a salary for five years and are happy to be driving equipment in the busy times of spring and fall. Other retiring farmers may take on the role of "landlord relations" for the farm team.

Some folks are so attached to their land and their "iron" that they are not capable of letting go or making new agreements with new tenants or owners. There is a huge issue in agricultural circles with "avoidance behavior," so if the fellow that you want to buy or rent land from crosses the street when you approach, you likely have damaged the trust relationship.

Notes:

_____

_____

_____

_____

_____

_____

_____

_____

_____

_____

HEALTHY HABITS

Chapter 28:

Causes (and Solutions!) for Procrastination

I'm sure you may have heard a farmer say, "Someday this farm will be his," or "Someday we will get to the lawyer's office, but we have work to do!" My sister Barbara Edie wrote the headline "someday is not a day on my calendar" when she relayed the memories of an active 1988 spent with my other sister Grace who died tragically that year. Barb's resolve was never to put things off, and not let "someday" creep into her thinking.

5 Causes of Procrastination

July on the farm used to be a great time for camping trips, visitors, weddings and stealing peas from the garden. Many folks today tell me that their July is now packed full of crop protection fungicides, off-farm work, and trying to find two or three nights off the farm. Folks hope to take time off..." someday!"

The word procrastinate formed from two Latin words – pro, meaning 'forward,' and crastinus, meaning 'belonging to tomorrow.' So, procrastination is the act of putting something into tomorrow and, of course, it suggests that it is always 'in tomorrow' – so it never gets done.

Why do we put things off, like special family times that we know only have a certain window of opportunity? Why do we delay plans to make our farm businesses healthier?

My speaker friend, Pierrette Desrosiers, says that there are five main causes of procrastination.

1. A lack of planning and vision.

2. Perfectionism

3. A rebellious spirit.

4. A quest for adrenaline, liking to work under pressure.

5. Don't like doing a particular task, acting like a "spoiled child."

How to Avoid Procrastination

My speaker friend, Hugh Culver, believes procrastination is about choices; it is not an innate characteristic of a person. "You are not a procrastinator," he says. You always get more of what you focus on. He calls us to re-frame our decision making, and start developing better decision-making habits.

Break Tasks into Steps

In farm families, I sense there is a huge sense of overwhelming, so people get stressed and just shut down. When I show up as a coach, we work to make an action plan that is realistic and which takes into account the steps along the way. For example, you know you need to update your will. The first step, find the old copy. The second step, call the lawyer for a first appointment. The third step, talk to your spouse and then book time to converse with your family. July is a good time to have some of these important conversations after family celebrations when you are just hanging out on the deck watching cloud formations.

Focus and execute was a mantra that caught my eye and has become a common expression for me. To establish a plan, you need to think about what goals you want to reach. Break things down into steps, and work out the timelines for execution. Deadlines work for me; if I post them in my computer calendar, I can keep them top of mind and move them along.

Reward Your Action

You can also avoid procrastination by building rewards into your tasks. For example, the reward for me as a writer to meet deadlines is that I get paid! What rewards can you build into the projects that you are avoiding?

One summer the junk (i.e. steel, augers, etc.) needed to be removed from our bush. Wes encouraged all the employees to participate in the project of loading the flat deck. Each employee's reward for this "not so fun" cleaning job was to have the money from their load, a little-added incentive not to keep stashing old equipment in the trees.

Decide to ACT, Not Avoid

Take the first step. Make the phone call for an appointment with the painter, lawyer, carpenter, plumber, doctor, etc. Moving it out of your brain and starting to take action will beget more action.

Perhaps this is the summer you have determined to look better in your bathing suit. This would be an ongoing project for me. My girlfriend Wendy said "Elaine you have written books, you are smart. You will start to lose weight when you decide it is important enough!" Don't you just hate it when your friends tell you the truth?

Decide to let go of perfection and just start the project. Weight loss is a classic procrastination issue, and farmers who are riding equipment, eating Saskatoon pie with lots of ice cream, and avoiding their doctors can relate to feeling bad about not dealing with their health.

It's Not What You 'Should' Do – It's What You WILL Do

Counselors use a phrase: "don't should on yourself." Rather than saying, "I should talk to my son and his wife about their vision for this farm," say "I am going to start having conversations about what is working for our family farm team, and what needs to change."

Choose Your Most Productive Times

Think about what time of day you have the best energy to do the hard work. As a writer, I like to have a 2-hour block of quiet time in the mornings. Once I get "in the zone," I don't answer the pings of my texts or the phone. What would it look like if you took 90 minutes this morning to tackle a tough project that you have been putting off?

Try a Team Approach

Would it help to have a buddy to help you on the tasks you have been procrastinating? Our seed plant office had a lot of mud this spring after 8 inches of rain and lots of traffic. When I started to try to find the floor, it did my spirit and energy level a lot of good to have a cleaning buddy.

My mom always used to say, "many hands make light work." Sometimes the work we are avoiding may be more fun with a team approach. I haven't been able to convince my family on this one with weeding the garden, but start that kind of training with young children, and you may have better results than I did!

Take some time this month to develop a "rallying cry" for getting things done. Make a list of things you've been procrastinating and start checking things off that list! And make sure to have fun with your family this summer. You should never put that off!

Notes:

_____

_____

_____

_____

_____

_____

_____

_____

Chapter 29:

Dealing with Stress on the Farm

Recently Mike Lipkin offered me a checklist of champions. This checklist encouraged me to think about what it takes to be a champion on the farm. From my thought process, I created a checklist of what might be creating tension on your farm when you don't feel like a champion.

Take a few moments for self-care and self-awareness to review the key points of this checklist. It will help you identify areas where you can creatively fix your "farm stress mess" this year.

The checklist is divided into stress from different sources, including family, money, health, personal tensions, and relationships. For each item on the list, place an X next to the ones where you are currently experiencing stress.

Farmer's Checklist of Champions:

Stress from Farming with Family

- ☐ Overall job dissatisfaction.
- ☐ No ability to make decisions because the founder won't let go!
- ☐ Questions about future job potential when there are no agreements in place.
- ☐ Stress over specific work projects.
- ☐ Feeling like there is too much to do and the farm's work is "never done."
- ☐ Deadlines (or lack of deadlines).
- ☐ Expectations of me are unrealistic.

- [ ] Education, when you would like more but don't know how to make it work.

- [ ] Inadequate communication with the farm team

Stress from Money and Finances

- [ ] Income is irregular, but we need to meet our family living needs.

- [ ] Overwhelmed by debts including credit cards, mortgage, debt for land, and operating loans.

- [ ] Retirement plans are nil.

- [ ] Cash flow/spending habits are an issue. We don't track our spending.

- [ ] Difficulty growing savings for the future and/or an emergency fund.

- [ ] Worry about planning for the future, and/or finding the financial experts to help

- [ ] Investments all go back into capital purchases for the farm, giving no personal wealth bubble.

- [ ] Living expenses/bills seem to be increasing with young children.

- [ ] Caregiving costs (or the refusal of aging parents to talk about the subject).

Stress from Heath Issues

- [ ] Overall health status is not where I would like it to be.

- [ ] Appearance could be improved.

- [ ] Weight has been an ongoing issue.

- [ ] Fitness is not happening. I need to walk and workout more.

- [ ] Current health challenges are impacting my sleeping patterns.

- [ ] Stress load will always need managing. I need more time for self-care.

- [ ] Mental well-being. Am I depressed? Should I ask my doctor for the test?

- [ ] Future health is a concern as my aging friends are getting sick.

- [ ] Management of chronic conditions.

Stress from Personal Tensions

- [ ] Time management. Difficulty focusing on and completing important tasks.

- [ ] Confidence regarding my ability to get things done/reach goals.

- [ ] Household management. How can I ask for more help or delegate tasks?

- [ ] Personal hygiene/upkeep. Grooming is slipping. Slob alert.

- [ ] Priorities/organization. I need to write my action plan down with deadlines.

- [ ] Is my faith growing with a connection to other believers and community?

- [ ] Making a difference/giving back to my community.

- [ ] Monitoring happiness, personal fulfillment, and emotional stability.

- [ ] Trouble finding a sense of balance.

Stress from Relationships

- [ ] Spouse/partner – are we working on making our relationship stronger?

- [ ] Are siblings in contact and do they understand our vision for our farm?

- [ ] Are parents transparent and sharing their future life chapter expectations?

- [ ] Are children engaged with farm chores and learning to be independent?

- [ ] Do we have extended family members to celebrate good times with us?

- [ ] Are friends' part of our weekly plans to stay connected?

- [ ] Do neighbors know they can ask for help? Do we appreciate each other?

- [ ] Are co-workers at the farm appreciated, engaged, and happy to be on the team?

- [ ] Are farm managers learning to let go and delegate responsibility to others?

Assessing Your Stress and Tension

In which category did you check the most boxes? This is your greatest source of stress and tension. Are your sources of tension mostly about relationships? Money? Health?

Now, look at the individual check boxes. In which areas do you feel the strongest tension? What are the five most stress-prone areas in your life?

Once you identify the main sources of tension in your life, you can start to work on them. Knowing which areas of your life need improvement will help you be more intentional about working on those areas. You can start by answering these few questions:

What do you want to let go of?

What do you want to hold on to?

What do you want to take on?

What do you want to move on?

As you work to deal with your stress, new paths will appear...new beginnings.

Notes:

_____

_____

_____

_____

_____

_____

_____

_____

_____

_____

Chapter 30:

30 Ways to Love Your Brain

Since becoming aware of the Amen Clinics' brain scans and treatment tools, I've been much nicer to my brain. I hope this year you too will consider practical tools to treat your brain better, so you can love your brain, and change your life.

Instead of chocolates this Valentines, cut the sugar and do more great things for your brain. The founder of the Amen clinic is Dr. Daniel Amen, and he has written a great book – *Change Your Brain, Change Your Life: The Breakthrough Program for Conquering Anxiety, Depression, Obsessiveness, Anger, and Impulsiveness*. His recommendations have helped thousands of people get healthier and lose weight, besides being more supportive to their brains.

Dr. Amen's 10 Tips to Love Your Brain

Want to take better care of your brain? Here are Dr. Amen's tips to consider for you and your loved ones.

1. **Keep learning something new every day.** How about 15 minutes to learn French or Spanish? Or ways to restore old cars? Or some other hobby you have been interested in learning?

2. **Dance.** Movement and cardio are great for getting more oxygen to your brain.

3. **Shut off the TV and do something!** Dr. Amen says that watching TV is a "no-brain" activity!

4. **Eat nuts instead of sugar.** How we feed our brains is important. I cut back on the Christmas baking this past year and opted for

peanuts and almonds as snacks instead. Buy mixed nuts instead of chocolates for Valentine's Day!

5. **Break the routine of your life to stimulate new parts of your brain.** Write a love note with your opposite hand, hug your wife in a new way, or shoot your rifle sighting with your other eye. Challenge your brain to make new connections!

6. **Drink more water.** Dr. Amen says that even slight dehydration can raise stress hormones that can damage your brain over time! Give hubby a metal water bottle so he drinks more water on the farm. I like to add lemon slices to my water as I work at my desk. Avoid artificial sweeteners, sugar, and caffeine. If you are addicted to coffee, you might want to start the withdrawal process as part of your love pact to your family.

7. **Omega 3 fatty acids found in fish, fish oil, and flaxseed can help boost brain function.** We are adding ground flaxseed to our protein shakes, cereal, and yogurt for breakfast. You grow flax, now grind it and eat it for your brain health!

8. **Give your wife a fruit basket of blueberries, strawberries, blackberries, cranberries, raspberries, oranges, red grapes, cherries, and kiwis.** These fruits are high in anti-oxidants which reduces the risk of developing cognitive impairment.

9. **Eat a rainbow of vegetables at the family supper table, and have a family conversation.** In my book, families that dine together do fine together! The best antioxidant veggies are Brussel sprouts, broccoli, beets, avocados, red bell peppers, and spinach. I have almost stopped buying iceberg lettuce, and am okay with the fact that my family calls me a "salad snob." Spinach is far more nutrient rich, and I can't wait until the garden grows again!

10. **Donuts are simple carbohydrates and cause brain fog.** Please stop serving them as the snack at farm events. Seriously. Spend the snack budget on veggie trays, yogurts, cheese, apples, bananas, and water with lemon or green tea. Almonds are expensive, but hemp heart snacks and peanuts would make a real impression with your clients!

Improve Your Brain & Overall Health – My List

As I reviewed Dr. Amen's list of ways to love your brain, I decided to create my own list too. These are specific actions you can take that will help not only your brain but also your overall health.

1. Wear a helmet on the ATV, bike, and snowmobile.

2. Think positive, healthy thoughts. Feed your mind great things.

3. Journal five things you are thankful for each night before sleeping.

4. Breathe fresh air deeply, and go for long walks every day.

5. Solve conflicts and deal with the tough issues ("the undiscussabulls™"). Seek peace.

6. Exercise to stimulate the happy hormones to your brain...endorphins.

7. Enhance your memory skills.

8. Make beautiful music a part of your life. Your playlist or your piano or guitar.

9. Take head injuries seriously, even minor ones. No more soccer ball head butting.

10. Take medications when needed, e.g. for depression.

11. Touch others often (appropriately...shoulder hugs are good)

12. Make beautiful smells a part of your life...soft soaps are great! Flowers, too!

13. Sing and Hum whenever you can. Whistling can't hurt either!

14. Stop trying to read other people's minds.

15. Stop smoking.

16. Wear your seatbelt.

17. Stop judging difficult people; try to understand how their brain might function instead.

18. Embrace your problems and get help to solve them with professional expertise.

19. Be intentional about the plans you have and want for your love and life.

20. Don't focus too much on what other people think of you.

I have a coaching friend who was kicked in the forehead by her horse. She figures it will take seven years of healing to get her back to her pre-accident status. Our brains are very plastic, and they grow and change based on how we treat them.

I think a lot of farm families would enjoy better social, emotional and physical health if they started paying more attention to the cells in their skull.

I also read the book *The Woman Who Changed Her Brain* by Barbara Arrowsmith-Young, which is great encouragement to folks with learning struggles. She runs a school in Toronto, so seek her out. For farm families dealing with stroke, you will enjoy the book *My Stroke of Insight* by Dr. Jill Bolte Taylor who rebuilt her brain from the inside out. As I have two friends who had strokes before the age of 60, this is also on my radar.

The books you read, and the people you meet will have a profound effect on your life – and your brain!

I wish for you to love yourself, love one another, and love your neighbor. We all get to make choices on how we show that love, so get started by loving your brain and see what changes transpire.

Notes:

_____

_____

_____

_____

_____

_____

_____

_____

_____

Chapter 31:

Sparking Friendships and a Sense of Community

Many young folks are eager to climb on the bright yellow school bus and see the friends they missed over the summer. Meanwhile, farmers are focused on getting a late crop off, praying for an open fall (autumn) and no frost until late October.

Once the busy season has ended, more jobs on the farm will appear as they always do, but what attention are you giving to your friends in your community?

The Importance of Community

Everyone needs loved ones beyond their family who will listen to their heart's cry and share the joys and sorrows of the season. Unfortunately, many farmers are neglecting to take care of the friendships they nurtured in their younger years. Friendships need time and energy to thrive and grow, just like your crops do.

In the next three months, what is your rallying cry to create deeper friendships beyond the farm gate? Without friends and an emotional support group, you risk becoming isolated, and mentally distraught. As a farm family coach, I have asked several farm men who they go to beyond their spouses, and they typically say "no one." This puts a lot of pressure on the spouse to meet needs that are sometimes better met by a community of people.

Don't miss out on the fun of fellowship with folks. Laughter is great medicine.

Friends can share their stories and help you realize that you are not alone in the challenges that may come up and the farm storms that may be brought your way.

Friends are great for fun, relaxation, renewal and leisure activities. They provide an excuse for a much-needed break from farm labor. Friends can provide fresh insights and give us an outside perspective on what is happening in our lives and our farms. They can act as sounding boards to bounce ideas off. Watching our friend's lives unfold, gives us new approaches and perspectives for families, marriages, parenting and farm activities.

Good friends can give both positive feedback and constructive criticism (gently with kindness) when we can't see it ourselves. Community relationships can reassure that we are not alone and that people care about us. They can help hold us up emotionally and in practical ways when the storms of life hit. In a community, the celebrations are sweeter, and the tragedies are more bearable.

What Happens if You Become Socially Isolated?

If people become socially isolated, they may lose a sense of what the range of "normal" looks like. Their world may become so small they are unable to see the possibilities that exist or, on the other hand, they may think their untenable situation is "normal." In several of the most conflicted farm families we have worked with, these off-farm relationships have been severed over time, and the families are left in isolation to sort through the troubles.

Community relationships can reassure us we're not alone, and that people care about us. They can help hold us up, both emotionally and in practical ways, when life's storms hit. In community, the celebrations in life are sweeter and the tragedies more bearable.

Taking Charge of Your Emotional Health

Relationships with friends and your community are an important part of staying emotionally healthy. However, sometimes people need professional help too. If you need counseling, consider calling your province's farm stress line to have a professional listener help you get clarity about what the next steps are for better emotional health. For example, Manitoba Farm, Rural and Northern Services offers many ways to connect and chat. Check out the website or call their line at 1-866-367-3276 for counseling or stress relief. Here are some other important numbers:

- In Alberta call 1-877-303-2642 the Alberta Mental Health Help Line

- In Saskatchewan call 1-800-667-4442, the Farm Stress line.

- In British Columbia call 1-800-784-2433 crisis intervention line.

- In any situation...call God. He is always online.

Perhaps you don't need a counselor. Maybe you just need a good hairdresser...you will talk, and you will leave looking good! Also, don't forget to get support from family and friends – both on and off the farm.

Questions for Reflection

Take a little time for self-reflection to assess how you are doing regarding friendships and connections with your community. Here are some questions to ask.

- If you were feeling worried about something, who would you call?

- If there was a tragedy, who would you call?

- If you wanted to go out for the evening, how easy would it be to find someone to hang out with?

- If you had really wonderful news, who would be delighted to hear this news?

- Who can you share just about anything with and not get the sense that they are judging you?

If the answer to each of those questions was your spouse or someone else in your farm family, it is a sign that you may want to branch out and develop (or re-open) relationships with people off the farm.

7 Ideas to Spark Friendships

Do you not have many friendships or community relationships outside of the farm? It's time to do something about that! Here are some ideas to get you started.

1. Take the first step and invite folks over.

2. Start a potluck group and hang out on a regular basis with other families.

3. Call your best friend from high school and share stories.

4. Stop by your neighbor's house to say hello.

5. Join an activity group like a book club, bowling league, dance, golf, or Bible study.

6. Volunteer with a new community group.

7. Let go of your farm job list and start making friendship more of a priority.

Notes:

_____

_____

_____

_____

_____

Chapter 32:

Retirement: A Time to Reinvent Yourself

"Retirement is an artificial construct, stop thinking about it. Think about reinvention instead. I know too many people in their sixties who have "retired" from their occupations and basically are sitting around waiting to die. There is no moral or religious code calling for the excitement of life to end before life ends."

-Alan Weiss (a consultant I highly respect.)

Reinventing Yourself

Recently at a farm family meeting of siblings, we were trying to analyze why the parents were so reluctant to let go of farm asset ownership. I suspect that one of the key factors keeping transition planning stuck is the fact that many farm men do not have an identity, role, or purpose beyond their decade's old role of "farmer."

Is your dad looking for permission to continue owning a pick-up that he can fuel with farm gas or diesel, and does he still want a few cows to keep "busy?"

My farmer and I bought an Ocean Kayak – one that requires that we fuel ourselves with our arm power. We have explored many of the local lakes and plan to have more adventures next spring and summer. We also made sure that the craft can support young children who would delight in using it as a floating dock.

In coaching terms, people let go of old habits and ways when they have something new to look forward to and do. What is it that you need to unlearn? What new things can you learn this year that would excite you enough to spend less time managing the farm as you transfer decision making to your successors?

Hobbies for Farmers

Here's a possible list of hobbies for farmers:

- Kayaking
- Golf
- Hunting
- Tinkering
- Volunteering to drive cancer care folks
- Leadership institute work
- Camping in Russia and training new leaders (Kingdom Ventures International)
- Building new homes for MDS (Mennonite Disaster Service)
- Politics – local or provincial
- Ag policy leadership
- Entrepreneur mentoring or new deal making
- Starting a completely new business
- Selling farm machinery
- Helping at auction sales
- Reviving a trade such as an electric work or welding
- Art. Or creating art from "junk"
- Oxbow historian clipping from the Producer

- Flying remote planes or real life-size planes

- Working with the poor in Haiti

- House parent in a teenage group home

- Fishing in winter and summer

- Teaching kids 4-H projects

- Emcee for community events

- Writing your life story

- Photo journaling, making memory books of photos of the farm

- Playing in a band that entertains many groups

- Driving seeders and combines

- Literacy classes at local school

- Recycling volunteer

- Flower planter and landscaper to keep the town beautiful

- Teaching English in a foreign country or in Brandon

- Refinishing furniture or repairing things for sale at the thrift store

- Baking (perfect for random acts of kindness and helping single moms)

- Cross country skiing

- Working in the food bank

- Feeding the birds, and building amazing feeders

I could go on and on. One of the great things about the internet is that you can Google "how to do…" anything, and come up with amazing ideas. You might also want to check out vocation vacations, elder volunteering, and chat with your local librarian. There are many workable ideas for all types of farmers.

Remember that you will have more excitement about getting out of bed in the morning when you feel that your life has purpose. Find out what "flow" is for you, the things that you do that make you lose all track of time because you are enjoying the activity to the max. I am in flow when I write, and when I paint watercolors. I also enjoy visiting.

If you need a push, start by de-cluttering your house or shop, then donating the things that you don't use or need anymore. That will create a new space and energy for a new hobby or latent hobby to be re-born.

Notes:

_____

_____

_____

_____

_____

_____

_____

_____

_____

Conclusion

I hope you have enjoyed the stories, advice, tools and encouragement found within the chapters of this book, which represents my journey as a farm coach throughout 2010 to 2016.

In that time, I have learned that Relationships, Communication, Teams & Operations, Planning, Succession, and Healthy Habits are the most common themes among my fellow farmers. In the end, we are all looking to cultivate loving and harmonious relationships on the farm, as we enjoy a tough but rewarding career in agriculture.

If you want more information and assistance on any of the themes or issues covered in this book, you may be interested in these additional resources:

Website: My website www.ElaineFroese.com offers more free advice, including blog posts and podcasts.

Farm Family Coaching: One-on-one sessions aimed at improving communication and conflict resolution skills on your farm.

Farm Succession Planning: Personalized help in creating a farm succession action plan and relieving your stress about succession.

Get Farm Transition Unstuck: An online course sharing tools to help move your farm transition planning forward.

Farming's In-Law Factor: A book filled with advice on how to ease conflict and create more harmony with in-laws on the farm.

Do the Tough Things Right: A workbook-style book that helps you identify and solve the communication problems on your farm.

Planting the Seed of Hope: An award-winning book of inspiration and encouragement for farm families.

Audio Lessons: MP3 files that address multiple topics, including succession, communication, stress and more.

Speaking: Powerful presentations for your next event, or view the calendar to see where you can hear me speak.

As a farm coach, I take great pride in helping farmers identify and address their unique challenges and work toward their personal farm goals. I wish you best of luck on your own journey, and should you need help along the way, please reach out to me at http://elainefroese.com/contact/.

Blessings on your journey.

Empower Family. Increase Profit. Secure Legacy.

More from Elaine Froese

Get Farm Transition Unstuck Online Course:

Get Farm Transition Unstuck is an online course designed for farm families who are ready for better communication that will help overcome the barriers that are keeping them stuck and without a transition plan. Learn more at: http://elainefroese.com/unstuck/

Private Coaching:

Elaine works one-on-one with farm families in her private coaching programs. To learn more about private coaching go to: http://elainefroese.com/farm-family-coaching/

Books:

Farming's In-Law Factor

Do the Tough Things Right

Planting the Seeds of Hope

Audio (MP3):

Who Gets the Farm and When

Ten Tools for Talking About Tough Issues

Planning for Change

Fixing Your Time Stress Mess

Leaving a Lasting Legacy

Don't Split the Yard

Books and audio files can be purchased at http://elainefroese.com/store/

Made in the USA
Columbia, SC
07 February 2025

52755304R00091